CONTENTS

FOREWORD

'In these, the twilight years of the nineteenth century, I am amazed at how high mankind has soared, and at how deep it has fallen, because of the myriad advances in our sciences and in engineering. Seldom does a day go by without a gentleman announcing his newest life-changing invention, each claiming it will benefit mankind in some way. It is a pity that we, the leaders of the civilised nations of the Earth, could not have put these marvels to better use. May God have mercy on us all.'

Robert Delamere, Lord Conway and Prime Minister 1893–95

It is 1895 and the world is in turmoil. In the decades to come historians will reflect upon the cause of this state of affairs and many will point at Charles Babbage. His perfection of the Difference Engine and then his Analytical Engine gave the new scientific establishments in the great imperial nations the tools they had so long needed in order to make a great leap forward. The ability to make huge and repeatable sets of complex calculations revolutionised the world.

Within twenty years came the perfection of miniaturised steam engines, electric lights and motors, Radium Bricks, Arc weapons, Hydrogen and, later, Helium Dirigibles, Road Trains, Calculating Artillery Engines, Sea and Land Dreadnoughts, and, well, the list is almost endless. Nothing is impossible when the wealth of a great nation is coupled to the unlimited imagination of educated men of science and their engineers.

The one thing that all these marvellous advances have not brought is peace. Every Great Power has been jostling its neighbours for resources and, more importantly, the latest technology. None can afford to stand still and allow its neighbours to advance their science and engineering unopposed, or they risk being overwhelmed as the French were in 1861 by the Prussians with the first Mobile Calculating Artillery Engines, or the Northern Americans in 1862, when their ports were put to the flame and successfully blockaded by the South's Armoured Sea Dreadnoughts.

Some nations have also been tapping into spiritual and psychic powers, producing an unholy union of the mystical and the mechanical, such as the ghastly Prussian Tod-truppen.

Although there have been relatively few open conflicts between the Great Powers, there is a state of undeclared and secret war between them all. This is where the Adventuring Companies come in. These are the deniable clandestine agents of the Great Powers (and of other globe-spanning organisations). They act in the shadows pitting their skills, their wits and the newest technologies against each other to obtain the latest scientific formula, artefact, or other vital component.

Small groups of highly skilled and specialised operatives are brought together for each mission under the command of a trusted leader. In Great Britain they work directly for Her Majesty's Government or out of

Akhenaton's forces clash with Lord Curr's Company amongst the ruins of the past.

IN HER MAJESTY'S NAME
STEAMPUNK SKIRMISH WARGAMING RULES

CRAIG CARTMELL & CHARLES MURTON

First published in Great Britain in 2013 by Osprey Publishing,
PO Box 883, Oxford, OX1 9PL, UK
1385 Broadway, 5th Floor, New York, NY 10018, USA
Email: info@ospreypublishing.com

Osprey Publishing is part of Bloomsbury Publishing Plc

A CIP catalogue record for this book is available from the British Library

Craig Cartmell and Charles Murton have asserted their right under the
Copyright, Designs and Patents Act, 1988, to be identified as the authors
of this book.

Print ISBN: 978 1 78096 289 4
PDF e-book ISBN: 978 1 78096 290 0
EPUB e-book ISBN: 978 1 78096 291 7

Page layout by PDQ Media, Bungay, UK
Typeset in Sabon and Myriad Pro
Originated by PDQ Media, Bungay, UK
Printed in China through World Print Ltd.

16 17   12 11 10 9 8 7 6 5

The Woodland Trust
Osprey Publishing is supporting the Woodland Trust, the UK's leading
woodland conservation charity, by funding the dedication of trees.

www.ospreypublishing.com

Acknowledgements

The authors would first like to thank the stalwart members of The Forge of War
Development Group for their inspiration and support. The enthusiastic way in
which they embraced the authors' earlier rules led to the production of this set.
In addition, they would like to thank that dastardly Prussian Matt Cook and their
doughty editor Phil Smith and his colleagues, without whom these rules would
never have seen print.

The editor wishes to thank Nick Eyre, Steve Saleh, Kev Dallimore, Dean Winsom
and everyone at North Star Military Figures for their incredible contributions to
this book.

the Explorers' Club in London's Pall Mall. In Prussia their patron is the highly secretive Thule Society and in the USA they are mostly sponsored by the Secret Service. There are similar organisations within each of the Great Powers. They all have the choice of their nation's latest arms, armour and other equipment with which to carry out their missions.

In Her Majesty's Name pits these small Adventuring Companies against each other in skirmish battles that may be single encounters or form part of longer narrative campaigns. The rules are quick to learn but have sufficient depth to give a satisfying evening's entertainment.

1.0 INTRODUCTION

This is a set of skirmish rules for games with two or more players with anywhere between five and twenty figures per side. The key design philosophy has been simplicity. The idea is that the players can learn the rules in a few minutes and then get on with the fun of fighting one another.

The game is based in the realm of the classic Victorian Science Romances and the more modern development of 'Steampunk'.

Each player forms an Adventuring Company led by a heroic officer, a devious foreign agent or one of a selection of other protagonists. They pit their forces against other Companies to advance the power and glory of their nations or causes – and perhaps for a handsome reward as well.

1.1 BUILDING A COMPANY

Each player in this game creates an Adventuring Company – a group of loyal comrades who follow a Leader.

A player has a set number of points to spend on his Company. We recommend that you start with between 250 and 300 points. After a few games, this can be increased to whatever limit you agree with your fellow players.

We have provided a selection of potential Companies for you to use (8.4), and also a complete points system (8.1) so that you can devise your own.

1.2 WHAT YOU NEED TO PLAY

Unlike many modern wargames rules, these do not require you to spend a huge amount of money to play a satisfying game.

As a minimum you will need five to twenty figures or counters per Company (and you will need at least two Companies for a game), a handful of ten-sided dice, a tape measure, the Reference Sheet from the back of this book and a flat space of about 3'x3' upon which to play.

There are many wargames and hobby companies out there happy to provide all this for you. Having painted figures and nice terrain does enhance the playing experience but is not absolutely necessary.

Lord Curr's Company, a fine body of men and women.

Regarding figures, our assumption is that these rules will be used with 28mm miniatures. If using other scales you can either leave the movement rates and ranges as they are or modify them as you see fit. If you do modify them, we recommend that you keep the proportions the same.

1.3 DICE CONVENTIONS

The only dice used in this game are ten-sided ones, which we call d10s. So, for example, if the rules require you to roll two ten-sided dice they will say 'roll 2d10', and so on.

Von Ströheim, Grand Master of the Society of Thule.

If the roll has a positive modifier the rule will say '1d10+' that modifier. So, if we are to add a positive modifier of two to the roll it will say '1d10+2'. Similarly a negative modifier of two would read as '1d10-2'.

A roll of one (1) on a d10 is always a failure regardless of how many modifiers you are able to add to it. Even the best of us have their bad days. The consequences of that failure will vary depending on what the roll was for.

1.4 MEASURING CONVENTIONS

It is considered bad sportsmanship to measure the distance between one of your figures and that of an opponent before deciding whether to shoot at them or move closer to them.

As a general rule, declare what you are going to do and only then measure.

Distances between figures should be measured from base edge to base edge.

1.5 THE GOLDEN RULES
COURTESIES

Each player should shake hands with each other player at the beginning and end of each game. A firm grip while wishing your opponents the best of luck is considered most acceptable.

This may seem strange but it establishes that this is a game for Gentlemen and Ladies, not scoundrels and yahoos.

CONDUCT BECOMING

This is only a game, and although having a certain level of passion is all well and good, intemperate language or behaviour is not the mark of a Gentleman or Lady.

Such phrases as 'Hear, hear!', 'Bravo Sir!', 'Play up, play up, play the game!', 'Tally ho!' and 'You are a dastardly fellow!' are perhaps the limit we aspire to achieve.

If one cannot do this then perhaps less port should be consumed before the game?

THE POWER OF RULES

Rules are for the obedience of fools and the guidance of wise men.

If there is a rule in this book that you and your comrades in arms do not like, or does not fit the scenario you are currently playing, then change it to suit.

However, do not do so unless everyone who is playing agrees to the change.

THE GENTLEPERSONS' AGREEMENT

If you encounter a situation in the game in which the rules don't seem to work and common sense seems to be in short supply, roll 1d10 and give an even chance to each possible outcome.

After the game, discuss the situation further and come a mutually acceptable ruling.

DECISIVE PLAY

This game is an evening's entertainment, not planning for the invasion of a foreign power. You should carry out your actions with a certain boldness so as not to delay the actions of your companions.

2.0 TROOP CLASSIFICATION

Every figure used in the game is defined by its attributes, armour, weapons and other equipment. Certain figures may also have unusual Talents or Mystical Powers.

Each of these has a points cost associated with it. These are covered in more detail in section 8.1.

2.1 ATTRIBUTES

A figure is defined by the following attributes:

PLUCK

This is a figure's inner reserve of courage, confidence, intestinal fortitude and even arrogance. To paraphrase Kipling, it allows them to keep their head when all about them are losing theirs.

It is the number the figure uses when rolling to save it from a hit that penetrates its armour, to charge a terrifying enemy or to resist certain Mystical Powers (3.5).

Lord Curr, a Gentleman. His Incorrigibles… less so.

SHOOTING VALUE (SV)

This is the bonus the figure gets when rolling dice in ranged combat. It represents the figure's aptitude, training and marksmanship when trying to hit an opponent from afar (3.3).

FIGHTING VALUE (FV)

This is the bonus the figure gets when rolling dice in close combat. It represents the figure's aptitude, training and instincts when things get up close and personal (3.4).

SPEED

This adds to the figure's base movement and modifies some attack rolls against the figure.

2.2 OTHER CHARACTERISTICS
TALENTS

Many figures may have one or more Talents (6.0). These are skills and abilities that give the figure certain advantages and options in the game.

MYSTICAL POWERS

These include all forms of magic or spiritual abilities, etc. (7.0). Though there are no specific limits, only a few figures in any game are likely to have Mystical Powers and some Companies won't have any at all.

2.3 EQUIPMENT

For simplicity's sake we advise that a figure is equipped with what you can see on it. This applies especially to arms and armour. However, you can agree with your comrades that a figure has different or additional equipment if you so wish.

    All figures are assumed to be competent with all of their equipment.

    Figures may not usually take and use equipment from other figures. Exceptions are grenades and rocket grenades (the latter only if the taking figure already has a Congreve Rocket Gun). Figures can also replace weapons that have become useless as the result of a Fumble (3.3.1 and 3.4.1) with another weapon of the same type.

    Example: Sgt Borrage's military rifle has jammed due to him Fumbling his Shooting attack. He can still use it to Fight with, but if he wants to Shoot again he will need to take a replacement military rifle from someone else. This could be a willing comrade or a fallen figure.

By the ninth day, Rutherford was starting to regret forgetting the compass…

3.0 PLAYING THE GAME

The game is played in a series of turns, each being divided into four phases: Initiative, Movement, Shooting and Fighting.

Throughout these rules we shall be using The Prince of Wales's Extraordinary Company (8.4.1) for most of the examples.

3.1 INITIATIVE

At the beginning of a turn each player rolls 1d10 and adds the Leadership bonus (if any) of the most senior member of their Company still in the game.

If two players have the same initiative score, roll again until the order of play is resolved.

Example: One player scores 12, two players both score 7 and the fourth scores a 5 for their initiative. The player who scored 12 will go first. The players that scored 7 roll again, adding their Leadership bonuses. The winner will go second and the loser will go third. If they tie again then, they keep rolling until they get different scores. The player who scored 5 goes last.

In each phase of the turn, the player who won the initiative gets to act first with one of his figures. Then the next highest can act, and so on in rotation, until all figures have acted in that phase.

3.2 THE MOVEMENT PHASE
3.2.1 MOVEMENT – GENERAL RULES

Each player may move each of his figures up to their maximum distance. For figures on foot this is generally 6" + Speed. Those on horseback or using other methods of transportation may have greater or lesser movement (5.4). Figures in Heavy Armour lose their Speed bonus (if any).

Any figure already engaged in a Fight cannot move other than to Disengage (3.2.4).

A figure may be moved in any direction. Its movement may be slowed by the terrain and/or visibility (4.1).

If a figure needs to scale a building or other upright terrain feature, measure the vertical distance as well as any horizontal movement. It is assumed that there is always a way up (ladder, stairs, pile of rubble etc.) inside the building unless the players agree that there is not.

Example: To ascend to the first floor of a ruined building that is 3" above his current position, Sgt Borrage has to use 3" of his movement.

A player can change his mind about where to move a figure – but only up to the point where he declares that he has finished moving, so that the next player in the initiative order may move one of his figures.

The Légion's advance meets with an unexpected obstacle.

3.2.2 RUNNING

A player may decide that, instead of a normal move, his figure will Run. This increases the distance the figure can move by 3". However, any figure that Runs during the Movement Phase cannot Shoot in the Shooting Phase of that same turn.

Figures in Medium or Heavy Armour (5.1) cannot Run.

3.2.3 MOVING INTO CONTACT

During the Movement Phase a player may, if they can move far enough, move one or more of his figures into base-to-base contact with figures from other Companies.

Figures in base-to-base contact with an enemy are engaging them in Fighting (3.4). Figures that are Fighting cannot move other than to Disengage (3.2.4).

Example: With his trusty sabre in hand, Captain Napier moves into contact with a native spearman. Sgt Borrage joins him to menace the native with his bayonet. The native doesn't like the look of this much – but he's already had his movement this turn so he'll have to stay put and face the music.

When a figure joins an existing Fight, the player owning that figure chooses which enemy it attacks. This can result in the existing Fight being split into separate Fights – these should be moved slightly apart to prevent any confusion. This will result in base-to-base contact being broken between the two fights.

Wherever possible, try to pair off combatants. This makes it a lot easier when resolving Fights.

Example: Somehow the native spearman survived a turn of Fighting with Captain Napier and Sgt Borrage. On the next turn, a second spearman comes to his aid. The newcomer chooses to engage Sgt Borrage, leaving the original spearman to face Captain Napier. There are now two separate Fights going on, each of them one-to-one. The player separates the two fights by a quarter of an inch. If a third spearman could reach these Fights he could choose which one to join.

3.2.4 DISENGAGING FROM A FIGHT

A figure can attempt to Disengage from a Fight provided that it has not already moved during the current Movement Phase.

An attempt to Disengage requires a Pluck roll (3.5.1) at a penalty of one for each opponent engaged with the figure. Success indicates that the figure can Disengage, failure that it is stuck in the fight this turn and cannot move. When Disengaging the figure moves normally but cannot move into contact with any other enemy figure during the current Movement Phase (though other figures may later move into contact with it).

Example: Captain Napier and Sgt Borrage have moved into contact with a single Boxer rifleman. Fortunately for the Boxer the Brits have moved before him. This means he can attempt to Disengage. His player tries to make a Pluck roll for him – but it's at a penalty of -2 because he's engaged by two opponents, so his chances aren't good. His Pluck is 6+, he rolls 1d10, gets a 7 and deducts 2 for a final score of 5, so he fails to Disengage.

3.2.5 MOVEMENT AND TERROR

If a Terrifying enemy (6.0) attempts to move into contact with a figure, a Pluck roll is required for that figure to stand its ground. Failure means

that the figure flees 1d10 inches directly away from the Terrifying enemy. It can deviate from a straight line only to avoid impassable or dangerous terrain and will be slowed by Difficult Terrain (4.1.1) in the usual way. It cannot come into contact with an enemy or move closer than 1" to one while fleeing. If for any reason the figure cannot move the full distance (i.e. it is blocked by enemies and/or impassable or dangerous terrain) then it moves only as far as it can.

Depending on its roll, and the proximity and speed of the enemy, the fleeing figure may still be contacted. Note that, regardless of how far it actually moves, a fleeing figure counts as having Run this turn – and therefore cannot Shoot in the Shooting phase.

If a player wants one of his figures to move into contact with a Terrifying enemy, a Pluck roll is required. Success means that the figure can move as desired – but failure means it cannot move at all this turn. It can still Shoot and, if contacted by an enemy, Fight.

3.2.6 MYSTICAL POWERS
Some Mystical Powers (7.0) can only be used in the Movement Phase.

A figure can use such a Power only at the beginning or at the end of its movement because it has to stand still for a moment and concentrate.

3.2.7 JUMPING
A figure using a Rocket Pack, a Vertical Spring Translocator (5.4) or other method of leaping over a distance may move as above but can ignore intervening terrain. The figure must begin and end its move on the ground.

A Figure that Jumps cannot also Run in the same turn.

If the Jumping figure attempts to take off or land in an area of Difficult Terrain, a Pluck roll is required at a penalty dependent on the terrain type (4.1). Failure means that the figure is Knocked Down (3.5.1).

If the figure attempts to land or take off in Dangerous Terrain, a Pluck roll is required at a penalty of -4. Failure means that the figure is out of the game.

3.2.8 FLYING
A figure using a Luft Harness (5.4), an Ornithopter (5.4) or other method of flying may move as above but can ignore intervening terrain.

A figure that is Flying cannot Run.

If the Flying figure attempts to take off or land in an area of Difficult Terrain, a Pluck roll is required at a penalty dependent on the terrain type (4.1). Failure means that the figure is Knocked Down (3.5.1).

If the figure attempts to land or take off in Dangerous Terrain, a Pluck roll is required at a penalty of -4. Failure means that the figure is out of the game.

Lord Curr and the Incorrigibles bravely charge Prussian Tod-truppen.

3.3 THE SHOOTING PHASE
3.3.1 SHOOTING – GENERAL RULES

The player with the highest initiative chooses one of his figures, selects a target that is in line of sight, checks the range and rolls to hit. The other players do the same, following the initiative order until all figures that can Shoot have had the opportunity to do so, assuming that they survive the attacks of figures higher up the initiative order.

A figure armed with a ranged weapon may Shoot at any enemy figure that is both in range and in line of sight.

Wherever possible, look along the line between the shooter and the target – if any part of the target can be seen then it is in line of sight, unless there is an area of terrain anywhere along that line of sight, in which case it may not be.

An area of terrain blocks line of sight to figures beyond it, and to/from any figures that are inside it and more than 3" from its edge. Inside Difficult Terrain (4.1.1), line of sight is 3".

Note: A small periscope can be very useful when checking line of sight but is not essential.

The player can check line of sight before selecting the targets for his shooting figure. This can be affected by twilight, fog, or darkness. However, he should declare his figure's target before measuring the range (1.4).

Range is measured from the nearest edge of the shooter's base to the nearest edge of the target's base.

For a vehicle-mounted weapon measure from the closest part of the hull of the vehicle, not the end of the weapon barrel. When shooting at a vehicle measure to the nearest part of the hull.

The roll to hit is: **1d10 + figure's Shooting Value (SV) + Weapon Bonus (5.2) + any other modifiers.**

Other modifiers may include adjustments for Terrain (4.1), Visibility (4.1), Moving and Shooting (3.3.2), Talents (6.0) or Mystical Powers (7.0).

If the modified score equals or exceeds the opponent's total Armour (5.1) then they are hit and must make a Pluck roll to stay in the game (3.5).

Example: Sgt Borrage and his section are advancing across a set of railway lines. Ahead of them are a group of five anarchists chanting slogans and preparing their fearsome Brick Lane Bottle Grenades under the cover of some coal heaps and railway sleepers. Sgt Borrage orders his Marksman, Private Davies, to engage the enemy while he and the rest of the section close on them. Davies drops to one knee and calmly takes aim with his Lee-Metford rifle. Choosing an anarchist with a battered top hat who is concentrating on igniting a grenade, he fires a single shot at him.

As a Marksman (see 6.0) Davies ignores the cover given by the stack of railway sleepers behind which the anarchist is hunkered down. The player rolls a 7, adds 1 for Davies' SV and another 3 for his military rifle for

Mohan Singh and the Incorrigibles, armed to the teeth.

a total shooting score of 11. The anarchist is wearing brigandine, making his total armour 9. A smoking hole appears in his tunic and unless he can make a Pluck roll he's out of the game.

If the d10 roll for the attack is a natural 1, the Shooter automatically misses, regardless of adjustments.

This is a Fumble and may have other consequences. Roll another 1d10. If the result is a second natural 1, the weapon is unusable for the rest of the game. If the Shooter is using an Arc, flame, explosive or poisoned weapon then the weapon makes an immediate attack on the Shooter before becoming useless – roll the attack using the weapon bonus but no other modifiers.

3.3.2 MOVING AND SHOOTING

Shooting at a figure that has moved at least 3" during the Movement Phase of the current turn incurs a penalty of -2 to Shooting rolls at it. If the target figure has Run, increase this penalty to -3.

A figure that has moved at least 3" during the Movement Phase has a penalty of -4 to its own Shooting rolls. If the figure has Run, it cannot Shoot this turn.

Mohan Singh, Lord Curr's loyal manservant.

Example: Sgt Borrage and the rest of his section moved closer to the enemy but didn't make contact this turn. They all shot, but the -4 penalty for moving while firing resulted in only one of the anarchists being hit. When shooting back, the anarchists suffered a penalty of -2 against any of the soldiers who had already moved this turn – so the best tactic was for each of them to Shoot at a soldier who hadn't moved yet (remembering that each player moves 1 figure at a time) or at Private Davies who didn't move this turn.

3.3.3 SHOOTING AT GROUPS OF FIGURES

If two or more figures are in base-to-base contact with each other, they form a group. Most ranged weapons can be used to Shoot at one individual in that group. However, if fired at a group a few weapons (e.g. machine gun, flamethrower) will make an attack against each member of that group.

If the group contains a mix of friendly and opposition figures, that means it's a Fight. When shooting into a Fight (other than with group-targeting weapons such as the flamethrower and machine gun), roll an attack at a penalty of -4 (in addition to any other adjustments). If the result is a hit, the intended target has been hit. If the result is a miss (but not a natural 1), determine randomly which figure has been targeted, then roll a fresh attack against that target without the -4 modifier. If this second roll also misses then the shot has missed the group completely.

Example: Reworking the previous example slightly, let's say that Sgt Borrage prefers cold steel. He therefore decided to Run and made contact with two of the anarchists. One of his soldiers fires at one of those two anarchists. The player rolls 6, adds 2 for the soldier's SV and 3 for his military rifle, then subtracts 4 because the target is in a Fight. The result is a 7, which is not enough to hit the anarchist who has an Armour of 8. The player now determines which of the figures in the Fight is the target of the wild shot. There are three figures in the fight so to split the odds evenly between them the player decides 1–3 will be Borrage, 4–6 the first anarchist and 7–9 the second anarchist. If he gets a 10 he'll re-roll. He rolls 7, so the soldier now gets an attack roll at the second anarchist, without the -4 penalty, which is resolved normally. He probably also gets a rollicking from his sergeant after the engagement!

3.3.4 SHOOTING WHILE IN A FIGHT

Figures in a Fight can Shoot at an opponent in the same Fight with one-handed ranged weapons **only** (i.e. pistols etc. – but not Arc weapons, see 5.2.2). If the opponent has a Speed then that is subtracted from the Shooter's attack roll.

Example: Captain Napier has his trusty sabre in his right hand and his Webley pistol in his left as he moves into contact with a native spearman during the Movement Phase. During the Shooting Phase he fires the Webley at the spearman. The native is unarmoured but very fast on his feet – he has a Speed of 2. Napier's attack roll is a 5 on 1d10; he adds 4 for his SV and 1 for the pistol, then subtracts 4 because he moved this turn and a further 2 for the native's Speed. Even though the native is unarmoured (and therefore has an Armour of 7), Napier's adjusted attack roll of 4 is nowhere near enough for a hit. However, if this was the second turn they'd been Fighting, Napier wouldn't have suffered the -4 penalty for Moving and Shooting – and the native would be trying to make a Pluck roll to survive the Webley bullet.

Figures in a Fight don't have to shoot at the figure that they are fighting, but they cannot Shoot at figures which are more than 3" away from them.

3.3.5 VOLLEY FIRE

A group of figures may choose to concentrate their Shooting in a single Volley at a single enemy figure. A single figure designated by the player as the 'primary Shooter' rolls to hit and, adds +1 to the roll for each extra friendly figure joining him in Shooting at the target.

Lady Felicity and the Incorrigibles fire a volley at a rampaging yeti.

This way, figures with relatively poor SV can join together to try to take down a well-armoured opponent, or perhaps one in hard cover. However, if they group their fire they will cause only one hit on their joint target. The hit, if achieved, will count as being from the primary Shooter's weapon.

Grenades, explosive weapons, flamethrowers and Arc weapons cannot be used as either primary or supporting weapons in Volley Fire.

Note: Each figure firing as part of a Volley must individually be in range and have line of sight.

Example: Mad Axe-handle McMurdo exits the Salisbury Provincial Bank, staggering under the weight of his Patent Kelly Suit and the sacks of gold coins he is carrying. Outside, Inspector Cholmondeley of Scotland Yard and four constables pepper McMurdo and the bank doorway with rounds to no visible effect. In return McMurdo blasts Constable Witherspoon with his shotgun. The brave inspector steps forward and cries, 'With me! Shoot his legs out boys!' As one, a volley of shots slam into McMurdo. This time the player only rolls for the Inspector, but adds +3 from the combined weight of fire of his remaining men. McMurdo drops as his knees are torn to shreds.

Note: Figures that engage in Volley Fire forgo their own attacks later in the Shooting phase, if they have not yet acted. A figure that has already had their attack in this phase cannot add to the Volley Fire.

3.3.6 MULTIPLE ATTACKS
3.3.6.1 GUNSLINGERS
Only a figure that has the Gunslinger Talent (6.0) may make more than one Shooting attack per turn, and then only if armed with two one-handed ranged weapons. The figure can make one attack with each such weapon; the figure's SV is divided between the two weapons with at least +1 allocated to each attack.

Example: Chris (a bald Gunslinger leading a seven-strong American Company of dubious characters) is armed with two Colt .45s and faced with a Prussian officer supported by a Tod-truppen. Chris decides that the officer is the bigger threat, so he splits his SV of +4 to give himself +3 against the officer and +1 against the Tod-truppen. His .45s give him +1 on each attack. There are no other applicable modifiers, so he will roll to hit the officer at +4 and the Tod-truppen at +2.

'Two-Gun Tess' demonstrates the aptness of her *nom-de-guerre*.

3.3.6.2 HEAVY WEAPONS
Figures armed with machine guns and flamethrowers can split their attacks. They may split their SV to make attacks against a number of target figures, but each figure targeted must be within 2" of the one before. This is called 'walking your fire'.

3.3.7 GRENADES
Attacks with grenades work slightly differently to normal Shooting attacks. The player whose figure is throwing a grenade designates a target spot on the ground and makes an attack roll. The SV of the thrower determines how far they can throw the grenade (3+SV"). Treat the point on the ground as a target with an Armour of 7 and roll the attack, adjusting for SV and other modifiers as normal.

If the attack roll is a miss then the grenade has disappeared down a hole, rolled behind some cover, or has not gone off because the pin was left in or is a dud. Grenades were notoriously temperamental in this period.

If the attack roll is a hit, a separate attack is rolled against each figure whose base is partly or fully within the grenade's effect radius (5.2.3). The thrower's SV is **not** added to these attack rolls. Neither are any adjustments for the thrower or targets having moved this turn. Other modifiers may apply, e.g. for terrain (4.1).

Example: One of the anarchists, a feared Incendiary, managed to get her Brick Lane Bottle Grenade (5.2.3) ready to throw just before Sgt Borrage and his section closed in. She can throw the grenade 3" +1" for her SV of +1, making a total of 4". The distance is measured and it's less than 4", so that's ok. She then makes an attack roll – and gets a 2. Adding +1 for her SV and +0 for the grenade gets her nowhere near the necessary 7. The grenade drops into a muddy puddle. Assume, though, that she did hit her target point and has caught two of the soldiers in the radius of effect. The anarchist's player now rolls an attack against each of those soldiers. The attack bonus from the grenade for this is +1 (5.2) and because it's a flame attack the soldiers' Armour is 7. There's no cover and it doesn't matter to the grenade that the soldiers were moving. The attacker scores a 5 and an 8 – so one of the soldiers got lucky and the other needs to make a Pluck roll. If he succeeds, he will also need to spend time rolling on the ground to put the flames out!

3.3.8 MYSTICAL POWERS

Some Mystical Powers (7.0) can only be used in the Shooting Phase.

A Power may enhance the figure's Shooting, count as a Shooting attack in its own right, or require the figure to forgo any Shooting attack in order to achieve some other effect.

3.4 THE FIGHTING PHASE
3.4.1 FIGHTING – GENERAL RULES

The player with the highest initiative chooses one of his figures that is in base-to-base contact with an opponent and rolls to hit. The other players do the same, following the initiative order until all figures that can Fight have had the opportunity to do so, assuming that they survive the attacks of figures higher up the initiative order.

The roll to hit is: **1d10 + figure's Fighting Value (FV) + Weapon Bonus (5.2) + any other modifiers.**

Other modifiers may include Talents (6.0) or Mystical Powers (7.0).

If the target figure has a Speed bonus then that is subtracted from the attack roll.

Note: Terrain has no effect on Fighting as the combatants are toe-to-toe.

If the modified score equals or exceeds the opponent's total Armour (5.1) then they have been hit and must make a Pluck roll to stay in the game (3.5).

Example: Captain Napier is still Fighting a native spearman. Napier's player rolls 4 on the d10, then adds Napier's FV of +4 and a further +2 for his sabre, then subtracts -2 for the native's Speed. The result of 8 is enough to hit the unarmoured spearman (Armour 7) who now needs to make a Pluck roll to stay in the game. He's been hit by a sabre, so there will be a penalty of -1 on that Pluck roll (3.5).

If the d10 roll for the attack is a natural 1, the attacker automatically misses regardless of adjustments.

This is a Fumble and may have other consequences. Roll another 1d10. If the result is a second natural 1, the weapon is unusable for the rest of the game.

3.4.2 MULTIPLE ATTACKS

Some figures are allowed multiple attacks in the Fighting phase. Any figure with a FV bonus greater than +1 can split that bonus against more than one opponent as long as he is in base-to-base contact with each opponent he wishes to attack. He cannot, however, make more than one attack against any one of his opponents.

Note: It is the FV that is split. The weapon bonus applies to each attack, as do any other modifiers, and the opponent's Armour counts against each attack as normal.

Example: Captain Napier is in contact with two Mahdists, so he could split his FV of +4. He could attack each one at +2, or choose to attack one at +1 and the other at +3. He might choose to do the latter if one of the Mahdists was using a shield. The +2 bonus he gets from his sabre applies to each attack, so his Fighting rolls are at +4 each, or at +3 and +5 if he decides to focus on the Mahdist with the shield.

Note: Wherever possible, try to pair off combatants. This makes Fights a lot easier to resolve.

3.4.3 OUTNUMBERING

Where there is more than one attacker against a single defender, roll each attack separately. However, unless the single defender can split his attacks (3.4.2), he must choose just one of the attackers to attack back.

Each of the attackers gets a bonus of +1 to his attack roll for Outnumbering their victim. Note that the bonus is only +1 no matter how many attackers Outnumber a figure.

A maximum of four figures can surround a single enemy, unless it is extremely large. For larger figures use common sense and agree a number. Figures wielding two-handed weapons count as two figures for determining how many figures can surround another.

The Dragon Lady's pet yeti closes on some unlucky Prussians.

Example: Both of the Mahdists attacking Captain Napier in the example above get this +1 to their FV for Outnumbering him.

Note: A figure only gets an Outnumbering bonus if he still has comrades standing and able to fight when he acts.

Example: In the example above one Mahdist may get the bonus but the other may not if, when his attack comes around later on in the phase, his companion has already been despatched by Captain Napier's excellent swordsmanship.

3.4.4 MOBBING

Where a player's figures outnumber an opponent, but he doubts their ability to hit it, he can choose to Mob that figure. A single figure, designated by the player as the 'primary Fighter', gets a bonus of +1 for each friend helping him take down that opponent.

When Mobbing a figure use the same rules as for Outnumbering above for determining how many can do so.

Example: A gang of cunning Mahdists have caught Captain Napier in the open. They surround him and, after a phase of fighting, find that they cannot penetrate his defences, losing two of their number to his expert sabre strokes in the process. In the next turn they decide to act in concert and Mob him. Instead of four Mahdists attacking individually at +1 each, one leads the attack, adding his own +1 to the roll and also +3 for the other three supporting Mahdists. Things look grim for the valiant captain.

Note: Figures that Mob an opponent forgo their own attacks later in the Fighting phase, if they have not yet acted. A figure that has already had their attack in this phase cannot add to the Mobbing.

3.4.5 MYSTICAL POWERS

Some Mystical Powers (7.0) can only be used in the Fighting Phase.

Such a Power may, enhance the figure's Fighting, count as a Fighting attack in its own right, or require the figure to forgo any Fighting attack in order to achieve some other effect.

The warriors of the Black Dragon Tong swarm towards the enemy.

3.5 THE PLUCK ROLL
3.5.1 PLUCK – GENERAL RULES

To make a Pluck roll simply roll 1d10 and try to equal or exceed the figure's listed Pluck.

Each time a figure is hit make a Pluck roll immediately.

This roll can be modified if the victim has been hit by one of the weapons marked with a Pluck penalty in the Weapons list (5.2). Such weapons are so debilitating or terrifying that they reduce the chance of the figure being able to continue. Some weapons, such as improvised weapons and unskilled unarmed combat, are very weak and actually give a Pluck bonus.

If the result is less than the figure's Pluck then it is out of the game, unless it receives rapid medical attention (3.5.3).

If the result is exactly equal to the figure's Pluck then it is Knocked Down (3.5.2). Lie the figure on its side.

A natural, i.e. unmodified, roll of 1 is always a failure. If the modified score would still have equalled or exceeded the figure's Pluck then it is Knocked Down, otherwise it is out of the game.

A natural roll of 10 is always a success, regardless of the figure's Pluck and any penalties to it, and the figure keeps going. There is no chance of it being Knocked Down in these circumstances.

Example: The Servants of Ra are in a skirmish with the Black Dragon Tong. One of the Dragon Warriors has just hit one of Akhenaton's cultists with a two-handed sword – which has a blade poisoned by the Dragon Lady's Venom power. The cultist has a Pluck of 6+. The two-handed sword imposes a penalty of -2 on his Pluck roll and the poison imposes a further -2 penalty. However, the cultist rolls a natural 10 – he is miraculously unharmed!

Note: Automatic success on a natural 10 applies only to Pluck rolls, not to any other d10 roll in the game.

3.5.2 KNOCKED DOWN

A figure which has been Knocked Down is stunned by the force of the blow or shot. Lie the figure down. It cannot act again in this turn. It cannot even defend itself and must rely on its Armour and Pluck to save it if subsequently attacked. While a figure is Knocked Down its Speed does not apply as a penalty to Shooting or Fighting attack rolls. Any Shooting or Fighting attack made against a Knocked Down figure gains a bonus of +2.

A Knocked Down figure can attempt another Pluck roll during the Movement Phase of the next turn. Regardless of any penalties or bonuses applied to the original Pluck roll that resulted in it being Knocked down, this new Pluck roll is unmodified. If the roll equals or exceeds the figure's Pluck, it can spring to its feet and carry on as normal. If it fails then it remains Knocked Down throughout that turn, though it can try again at the beginning of each subsequent turn.

If a figure that springs back up is in base-to-base contact with an opposing figure then it remains in a Fight.

Example: Captain Napier has a Pluck of 3, but the Mobbing Mahdists managed to hit him with a spear, which imposes a penalty of -1 to the Pluck roll – and he rolled a 4. This adjusts to 3, which is equal to his Pluck, so he's Knocked Down. Next turn, though, he rolls a 3, but this time that's enough for him to spring back up and carry on Fighting.

Dr Kobalt leaves nothing to chance and finds as much cover as he can.

3.5.3 MODERN MEDICINE

Some Companies are able to deploy Medics (6.0). If they can get to an 'out of the game' figure before the end of the next Movement phase they can attempt to revive it. They can also improve the chances of a Knocked Down figure springing back to its feet.

The Medic must move into contact with the fallen figure during the Medic's next Movement phase. The Medic then spends the rest of the turn tending to the figure and therefore cannot Shoot or Fight during that turn. At the beginning of the following turn's Movement Phase the downed figure attempts another Pluck roll (with no modifiers) and if it **exceeds** its Pluck then it springs back up into the fray. If the Pluck roll is less than or equal to the figure's Pluck then it is definitely out of the game and there is nothing else the Medic can do.

Example: During the Shooting Phase, Sgt Borrage is hit by a well-aimed shot from a Prussian jäger and fails his Pluck roll. He's out of the game. Or he would be, were it nor for Doctor Wilson. At the start of the next turn, the good Doctor moves into contact with Borrage's slumped form and attempts to revive him. At the start of the following turn, Borrage gets to try another Pluck roll – this time he succeeds and gets back to his feet ready to go looking for that damnable Prussian.

If the figure has been Knocked Down, there is no time limit for the Medic to help it. At the start of a turn when the Knocked Down figure attempts to make its Pluck roll, the Medic can also attempt to make his Pluck roll. If either of them equal or exceed their Pluck, the Knocked Down figure can get back up.

Example: Reworking the previous example, when he was hit by the jäger's bullet Borrage made his Pluck roll exactly and was Knocked Down. At the start of the next turn, he tries to make a Pluck roll to get up, but fails – the pain from his injury is too much. Doctor Wilson rushes up to him and administers emergency first aid. At the start of the following turn, Borrage and the good Doctor both attempt Pluck rolls – if either of them equal or exceed their respective Pluck then Borrage is back on his feet again.

Note: A Medic cannot tend to a figure that is in base-to-base contact with an opposing figure.

3.5.4 POST-GAME SURVIVAL TEST – OPTIONAL RULE

You may wish to use this rule if you are running a campaign or league.

For each figure taken out during the game make a Pluck roll. If the roll exceeds their Pluck then they were just wounded and can return for the next game.

If they roll their Pluck exactly then they were seriously wounded and must miss the next game, but can return in the game after that.

If they fail the roll then they are dead.

Some characters are an exception to this rule – see the Immortal Talent (6.0).

4.0 SETTING UP A GAME

4.1 TERRAIN

This is a game that benefits from having plenty of terrain. It gives cover, blocks lines of sight and allows the players to manoeuvre their Companies in a satisfying and tactical manner.

If you don't have much terrain, don't worry. Remember, the recommended playing surface is only 3'x3'. When starting out, a few boxes will do, laid out in an approximate street pattern. There are also many artists on the web now offering cheap, or even free, downloadable paper terrain.

When laying out terrain, consider the scenario that you wish to play. Is it the streets and alleyways of the East End of London, a country manor and village in the heart of England, or something more ambitious? Many examples, including the benefits and hazards of each type, are listed in section 10.0 – Landscapes.

There are a number of factors you should consider when placing terrain on the field of play – these are listed below. All players should agree the effects of each piece of terrain before the game begins.

Sense and satisfaction: as a principle, terrain should be laid out in a fashion that makes sense of the landscape and gives you a feeling of satisfaction once completed. Even in competitive games a well-laid out table adds a lot to the gaming experience.

4.1.1 DIFFICULT TERRAIN

Difficult Terrain imposes restrictions on Movement depending on the figure or vehicle type attempting to traverse it. It also restricts visibility and may provide physical cover against Shooting.

In this game, Difficult Terrain is rated as Type 1, 2 or 3 – the number corresponds to the level of penalty associated with it. For example, Shooting at a figure behind an impromptu barrier (terrain Type 2) would be at a penalty of -2 on the attack roll.

In situations where the visibility is limited by fog, twilight or darkness the terrain type increases by one. Thus Dense Woodland being Type 2 would become Type 3 in fog and normal terrain would become Type 1 Difficult Terrain. Note that, regardless of the combination of terrain and visibility, the attack penalty is never worse than -3.

Type	Terrain Examples
1	Open woodland, fences, low walls, wooden buildings, streams, tall crops, sand dunes
2	Dense woodland, mud brick buildings, log buildings, ditches, shallow rivers and their banks, piles of junk, impromptu barricades, henges, hedgerows
3	Trenches, bunkers, solid brick or concrete buildings, iron bridgeworks, railway locomotives, ship bulkheads, dense jungle, rocky outcrops and tors

With their backs to the jungle, Lord Curr's Company holds off the native horde.

4.1.2 LINEAR TERRAIN

This consists of rivers, canals, rail tracks and roads. Natural terrain such as rivers should normally run from one edge of the board to another. Man-made linear terrain can cut through other terrain features using bridges, viaducts etc. as appropriate; it can also terminate on the board.

The late Victorian era was one in which the transport infrastructure was being laid, without let or hindrance, as fast as people and corporations could get it done. Lines of communication across games tables should therefore be common.

The Society of Thule skirts an area of impassable terrain.

4.1.3 IMPASSABLE TERRAIN

Some terrain is just impossible for ground-based figures or vehicles to traverse. This includes deep and fast rivers (except at bridges), deep chasms, cliffs (such as in quarries), lava flows, lakes etc.

Some Impassable Terrain (e.g. a cliff) may completely block lines of sight, and therefore block Shooting as well as Movement. Other Impassable Terrain will have no effect on lines of sight or Shooting. Players will need to agree the full effects of each piece of Impassable Terrain before play starts.

4.1.4 ACTIVE TERRAIN

Some types of terrain move and may interact with the figures as they fight their way across it. Examples include:
- Railways – engines, carriages etc.
- Road traffic – carts, wagons, omnibuses, trams.
- Quarries and mines – mine carts and engines, conveyor belts.
- Factories – conveyor belts, lifts, cranes.

It is recommended that each of these should move along a preset path at a random movement rate of 1d10" or 2d10" per turn. This movement should be carried out at the end of the Movement Phase and may create exciting situations as figures suddenly find themselves in the path of something potentially lethal.

4.1.5 DANGEROUS TERRAIN

This is terrain that may well not react well to being damaged. For example:
- Coal gas or hydrogen gas tanks.
- Crates full of explosives/ammunition.
- Canisters of poison gas or toxic chemicals.

If you miss when Shooting at a figure within 3" of a piece of Dangerous Terrain, or include it in an explosion or flame attack, then there is a chance that it will react.

At the beginning of a game rate each piece of Dangerous Terrain from 2 (incredibly dangerous) to 9 (slightly dangerous). When there is a risk of setting the item off, roll 1d10; if you score equal to or higher than the rating the Dangerous Terrain explodes, automatically causing a hit on every figure within 6". Each figure is Knocked Down and must make a Pluck roll to avoid being taken out of the game.

4.1.6 SETTING UP TERRAIN
There are three recommended methods for setting up terrain:
1. Dice to see who chooses terrain. The winning player places all the terrain. Once it is set, the other players can veto up to an agreed number of terrain pieces each and either remove them entirely or move them up to 6" in any direction.
2. Terrain Purchase. Each player gets an agreed number of terrain points. Each piece of terrain can measure no more than 9" in any direction, including vertical. An area of Difficult Terrain costs 1 plus its type (4.1.1) in points. Impassable and Active Terrain costs 5 points. Dangerous Terrain costs 10 points. Players roll for initiative (3.1), and then take turns to choose and place terrain until all of it has been used.
3. The players cooperate in producing a pleasing and suitable terrain set-up, perhaps referring to the Landscapes described in section 10.0.

4.2 DEPLOYMENT
Some scenarios (9.0) define where the participating Companies can be deployed. Otherwise, the players should agree a number of starting locations on the table edges equal to the number of participating Companies. Once this has been done, the players roll 1d10 (re-rolling to break ties) to establish a deployment order. The winning player chooses one of the defined starting locations and deploys one of his figures within 6" of that point. Then the next player follows suit, then the next, until all players have deployed all the figures they wish to have on the table.

Unless the scenario says otherwise, any player may hold back some of their figures and deploy them onto the table (within 6" of their Company's original starting location) as part of any Movement Phase later in the game. Such figures deploy but do not actually move during the phase they arrive on the table, though they count as having moved for the purposes of Shooting and Fighting. However, a player must (unless the scenario says otherwise) deploy at least half of his figures at the start of the game.

5.0 THE ARMOURY

5.1 ARMOUR
The ratings and costs of different types of armour are shown in the tables below.

Armour (ordinary)	Weight	Rating	Cost	Notes
None, just clothing	Light	7	0	What most civilians will be wearing.
Jack / Lined coat	Light	8	1	Leather and silk tunic or long coat, stiffened to protect vital areas.
Brigandine	Light	9	2	Tunic with padding and steel plates in vital areas.
Chain shirt, steel	Light	10	4	Light chainmail tunic over a padded shirt.
Breastplate, steel	Medium	11	9	Solid fitted steel, front and back.
Breastplate, SRC	Medium	12	16	Solid fitted steel-reinforced ceramic (SRC).
Plate armour	Heavy	13	25	Full head-to-toe gothic plate.
Shield	–	+1	*	This adds to any other armour worn. Occupies one hand. Used mostly by primitives.

Armour (extraordinary)	Weight	Rating	Cost	Notes
Faraday coat	Light	8	5	11 against arc weapons.
Faraday shield	–	+1	*	+3 against arc weapons, +6 if figure did not move this turn (and could stick the earthing spike into the ground). Occupies one hand.
Vulcan coat	Light	8	2	This is an ablative coat. The wearer automatically makes its first Pluck roll against a fire attack but this destroys the coat.
Patent Kelly Suit	Heavy	15	49	Updated version of plate armour, made from SRC.
Magneto-static waistcoat	Light	9	2	Creates a repulsion field around the wearer. Cannot be worn with Faraday coat or Shield as these earth out the field.
Magneto-static projection barrier	–	10	4	Affects all figures with 8". Requires a power source. Has no effect on figures with a personal Armour Rating higher than 10.
Magneto-static umbrella	–	+2	*	This adds to any other armour worn. Creates a personal repulsion field. Cannot be used with Faraday coat. Occupies one arm.

NOTES

Light armour imposes no restrictions.

Medium armour prevents a figure from running.

Heavy armour prevents a figure from running and nullifies any Speed bonus it may have.

A weight of '–' indicates an item which can be used with other armour.

* indicates an item of armour which provides protection that can be added to other forms of armour. To calculate the points cost, look up the total Armour Rating on the Armour costs table (8.2.4).

Breastplate armour. This looks like traditional medieval armour but is made from modern steel and provides enhanced protection. Those Companies with access to the latest technology may have steel-reinforced ceramic (SRC) breastplates, which are even better.

Brigandine armour. Typically made from tough materials like leather and canvas, this clothing (which can otherwise appear fairly normal) has steel reinforcements sewn into it to protect vital areas.

Faraday coat. A heavy leather coat with a fine copper mesh built into the lining. It provides light physical protection to the wearer – but more importantly it is one of the few forms of protection against Arc weapons. Faraday coats come in many styles and indeed are now available from the best gentleman's outfitters on Saville Row.

Jack / Lined coat. This covers both simple leather armour and perfectly ordinary looking clothes which have been modified to provide a little extra protection. The latter are favoured by gentlemen such as Lord Curr – after all, one wouldn't want to look inappropriately dressed.

Magneto-static umbrella. A hand-portable device that generates a repulsion field. This provides a degree of protection against physical attacks – bullets, knives, etc. – but not against Arc weapons or flamethrowers.

Magneto-static waistcoat. A wearable device that provides similar protection to the umbrella above.

5.2 WEAPONS

Most ranged weapons have enough ammunition to last the game. The exceptions are blunderbusses (which can be fired only once) and grenades (both thrown and rocket) which are one-use weapons and must be purchased individually.

Fighting (ordinary)	FV Bonus	Hands Required	Pluck Modifier	Cost	Notes
Unarmed (basic)	+0	1	+1	0	Brawler, pugilist, wrestler etc.
Unarmed (Martial Artist)	+1	0	+0	3	Karate, jiu-jitsu, kung-fu, savate etc. (cost is for Talent)
Improvised weapon (small)	+0	1	+1	0	Bottle, pistol butt, etc.
Improvised weapon (large)	+0	2	+0	0	Spade, chair, rifle butt, etc.
Bullwhip	+0	1	-1	2	
Club	+1	1	+0	2	Shillelagh, police truncheon etc.
English All-Electric Truncheon	+1	1	-1	3	
Nightstick	+2	1	+0	3	Also Japanese tonfa
Quarterstaff	+3	2	+0	4	
Knife	+1	1	+0	3	Small sheath knife; can be thrown
Knife (combat or fighting)	+1	1	-1	3	Large blade, e.g. bayonet, Bowie knife, kukri; cannot be thrown
Rapier	+1	1	-1	3	Includes swordstick
Axe	+1	1	-1	4	Hand axe; can be thrown
Axe (large)	+2	2	-2	5	Greataxe
Spear	+2	2	-1	5	Can be thrown. (e.g. Assegai)
Sabre/Sword	+2	1	-1	4	Military sword
Sword (large) or Halberd	+3	2	-2	6	Two-handed sword or polearm
Rifle & bayonet (military rifle only)	+3	2	-1	–	Only usable with Bayonet Drill (6.0). You must first pay for a military rifle (9) and a bayonet (3)

Fighting (extraordinary)	FV Bonus	Hands Required	Pluck Modifier	Cost	Notes
Steam fist / claw	+4	2	-3	8	Requires steam power source; often fitted to Boiler Suit or Walker.

Shooting (ordinary)	SV Bonus	Range	Hands Required	Pluck Modifier	Cost	Notes
Improvised thrown weapon	+0	3"	1	+1	0	Chair, rock, bottle, etc.
Thrown knife	+1	6"	1	+0	3	
Thrown axe	+1	6"	1	-1	4	
Thrown spear	+2	9"	1	-1	5	
Bow	+2	12"	2	+0	4	
Crossbow	+2	18"	2	-1	6	User must take a Shooting phase to reload, so can only be fired every other turn
Pistol	+1	9"	1	+0	3	Usually a pistol (e.g. Colt .45) but can also be early semi-automatic
Shotgun	+2	12"	2	+0 / -1	5	-1 Pluck applies within 9"
Shotgun (short)	+2	9"	1	+0 / -1	5	Sawn-off or shot-pistol. -1 Pluck applies within 3"
Blunderbuss	+3	6"	2	-2	5	Only good for one shot per game – takes too long to reload. If fired into a group attacks all targets equally
Carbine	+2	18"	2	+0	5	Small rifle using pistol ammunition. Magazine fed – usually bolt or lever (e.g. Winchester) action but can be semi-automatic (e.g. Mauser C96)
Muzzle-loading rifle	+3	18"	2	-1	6	(e.g. Jezzail) Can only be fired every other turn – need to spend a Shooting phase reloading
Military rifle	+3	24"	2	-1	9	Bolt or lever action, magazine-fed
Hunting rifle	+4	36"	2	-2	16	As used for big game such as lions, bears, buffalo and elephants. Can only be used to full effect by a figure with the Hunter Talent, otherwise Shoots as a military rifle
Machine gun	+5	30"	4	-2	15	Gatling or early water-cooled (e.g. Vickers, Maxim). Attacks can be split between multiple targets. If fired into a group attacks all targets equally (see 3.3.3)
Flamethrower	+2	9"	4	-1	11	Large fuel tanks and projector nozzle. Makes flame attack which can be split between multiple targets. If fired into a group attacks all targets equally (see 3.3.3)
Grenade (explosive)	+0	3+SV"	1	-1	6	Attacks all figures in 2" at +5 (ignore thrower's SV) (see 3.3.7)
Grenade (gas)	+0	3+SV"	1	-1	6	Automatically hits all figures within 3" of impact point with poison (see 3.3.7)
Grenade (Brick Lane Bottle)	+0	3+SV"	1	-1	6	Flame attack at +1 on all figures in 3" (ignore thrower's SV) (see 3.3.7)

Shooting (extraordinary)	SV Bonus	Range	Hands Required	Pluck Modifier	Cost	Notes
Arc pistol	+1	6"	1	-1	7	See Arc Weapons (5.5.2)
Arc rifle	+1	18"	2	-2	9	See Arc Weapons (5.5.2)
Arc cannon	+1	24"	4	-3	12	See Arc Weapons (5.5.2)
Congreve Rocket Gun	+3	18"	2	-1	7	Fires rocket-propelled explosive or gas grenades, each of which must be purchased separately and costs 1 point more than a standard grenade

5.2.1 HANDS REQUIRED

Any figure may simultaneously wield two one-handed weapons – but no more.

If a figure wields a two-handed weapon then that must be its only weapon.

Four-handed weapons normally require two figures to Move and Shoot. Neither figure may fire any other weapon, nor engage in Fighting, while using a four-handed weapon. Unless it has the Strongman Talent (6.0), a figure using a four-handed weapon on its own can either Move or Shoot during a turn, not both.

A figure may switch freely between its weapons.

Example: Lord Curr is carrying a hunting rifle, a pistol and a bullwhip. He can Shoot with the hunting rifle during one phase, then in the next phase he can move into contact with an enemy figure, Shooting with the pistol and Fighting with the bullwhip.

5.2.2 ARC WEAPONS

Available in pistol, rifle and cannon forms, these weapons shoot what is effectively a controlled lightning strike at their target. Normal armour provides no defence against this, though there are ways to protect against it (e.g. Faraday coat).

Arc weapons aren't usable in close combat (as there is too much danger of sharing the shock) and are slow to shoot. This is because they only hold enough charge for a single shot and then have to be recharged via a hand-crank mechanism, which takes a turn. If they are within the field of an Arc Generator, however, they recharge quickly enough to be fired every turn.

Unless otherwise stated in the Armour table above, Arc weapons ignore armour, so all targets have an Armour rating of 7. Other modifications to attack rolls, such as Difficult Terrain, still apply.

5.2.3 FLAME WEAPONS

Flame attacks are made using inflammable liquids, either shot from a flamethrower or bursting from a Brick Lane Bottle Grenade. Such attacks treat all figures as unarmoured, i.e. having an Armour rating of 7. Other modifications to attack rolls, such as Difficult Terrain, still apply. Once a figure has been hit by a flame attack, it must take a full turn (no Movement, Fighting or Shooting) to extinguish the flames. For each turn it doesn't do this, it must make another Pluck roll at the end of its turn. A Vulcan coat (5.1) provides one-off protection against these fearsome weapons.

5.2.4 POISON

Poison can be applied to all cutting Fighting weapons and to penetrating Shooting weapons except firearms. It imposes a -2 penalty on the Pluck roll for any hit by the weapon which is cumulative with any penalty imposed by the weapon itself.

Example: Private Davies is engaged in a Shooting match against several opponents armed with crossbows. His military rifle is a superior weapon, but the crossbowmen have poisoned their ammunition. If Davies is hit his *Pluck* roll will be at a penalty of -1 for the crossbow and -2 for the poison, making a total of -3.

Poison can also be used in gas form, in which case the Pluck penalty is -1. Poison gas lingers and immediately affects any figure moving into it – though it is clearly visible. If there is any significant wind then the gas will disperse at the start of the next turn, if not then roll 1d10 for the number of turns it remains. Limited protection against poison gas can be obtained from a Breath Preserver (5.3).

Whether the poison is lethal or sedative makes no difference to the game being played; sedative poison guarantees that the figure survives the experience and is automatically available for the next game in a campaign.

To poison a weapon costs 8 points.

5.3 WEIRD SCIENCE

There are literally thousands of discoveries and inventions in this period but only a relatively small number are suitable for inclusion in combat. Below are just a few.

Item	Description	Cost
Electrostatic Burst Generator	May be triggered once per game. All figures within 8" are hit with an electrostatic burst, suffering a d10+2 attack. Any figures that are hit are immediately Knocked Down but are otherwise unharmed. Owners of Arc weapons and devices within this radius must make a Pluck roll to avoid these items being rendered inoperable for the remainder of the game. Figures in Faraday coats are immune.	15
Monocular Targeting Array	Grants a +1 bonus to a figure's Shooting rolls.	7
Steam Dynamo	A portable device that provides mechanical power for weapons and equipment that require it. Figures equipped with this cannot Run.	10
Arc Generator	A heavy device, usually worn as a backpack, that generates an electrical field from which various devices – including Arc weapons and Tod-truppen – can draw power provided they are within 8" of the generator. The carrying figure cannot Run. If the carrying figure is Knocked Down, the Arc generator continues to function. If the carrying figure is taken out of the game, make a further Pluck roll for it – if successful the Arc generator survives and may be picked up by someone else. N.B. it is perfectly possible for an enemy to draw power from your Arc generator if he is standing within its field!	20
The All-Electric Limb Prosthesis	Grants a +1 bonus to a figure's Fighting rolls and +1 to its Armour rating. Requires an Arc Generator.	10
Breath Preserver	Early gas mask, looking much like the canvas-and-hose devices developed during World War I in the 'real' world. Gives +2 on Pluck rolls against poison gas.	2
Carbide Lamp	Provides light in a 6" radius. It takes a Shooting Action to light and can be extinguished at will.	3
Storm Lantern	Provides light in a 3" radius. It takes a Shooting Action to light and can be extinguished at will.	2
Revivifier	Allows a fallen soldier to rise again as a Tod-truppen. Only available to the Society of Thule.	5

5.4 PERSONAL TRANSPORTATION

There are numerous methods of traversing the battlefield from walking to flying. Each has its advantages, disadvantages and costs as described below.

Type	Description	Base Speed	Difficult Terrain?	Considerations	Cost
Ape Howdah	Trained giant Ape carrying a basket containing passenger	9"	No effect on Movement	See 8.4.2 The Explorers' Club	30
Bicycle	Two-wheeled transportation	9"	No	Needs one hand to steer	3
Edison Beam Translator	Transports one person across open space to a location they can see	n/a	No	Very heavy, reducing foot movement by 3". Takes one full turn to recharge from an Arc Generator	25
Horse	Trained mount	12"	Yes	Armour 8, Pluck 6+. Horses can be targeted instead of their riders. If a moving horse is Knocked Down or taken out of the game, the rider must make a Pluck roll. Horses can leap over low walls, fences and hedgerows if moving at full speed for no loss of distance.	5
Luft Harness	A personal dirigible that lowers and lifts its operator	4"	Ignores	Needs one hand to operate	10
Rocket Cycle *	Bicycle fitted with a one-use speed-boosting rocket	18"	No	Needs one hand to steer. Rocket-boosted movement is in a straight line only	8
Rocket Pack	A one-use jumping device	12"	Ignores	Can only go 12" – no more, no less	5
Shanks' Pony	Walking on your own two feet	6" + Speed	Yes		0
Steam Hansom *	A speedy modern horseless carriage for two passengers	12"	No	A driver with Pluck 6+, +0 SV and +0 FV is included in the cost of this vehicle. The driver can be upgraded for additional points (8.1) but can take no other action during a turn in which the vehicle moves	12
Steam Carriage *	A modern horseless carriage for four passengers	9"	No	As Steam Hansom. Furthermore, some Companies have experimented with armoured versions, adding armour (rating 11) and heavy weapons such as machine guns. To deploy one of these, add 9 points to the base cost, plus the cost of any weapons. Instead of a weapon the players may consider fitting it with an Arc Generator…	10
Ornithopter *	Flies one person around	9"	Ignores	Fragile – will crash if hit. Needs one hand to steer	20
Electro-trike *	An electric tricycle	12"	No	Needs one hand to steer	5
Vertical Spring Translocator	A reusable jumping device	12"	Ignores	Can only be set in 3" increments	8

The *Ophelia*, pride of Scotland Yard.

* If these Armour 7 vehicles take a successful hit, roll on the following table:

1d10	Effect
1–4	Driver or passenger hit (roll randomly) – roll Pluck as normal. If the driver is put out of action the vehicle ceases to function until he recovers or is replaced by someone else.
5–8	Vehicle is immobilised and cannot be used again this game. An immobilised Ornithopter makes a controlled landing immediately below its current position.
9–10	Vehicle is destroyed – each passenger must make a Pluck roll to get clear before it explodes (unless the vehicle was in the air, in which case everyone on board is out of the game and the vehicle crashes to the ground directly below, where any figures in the immediate vicinity are assumed to move out of the way automatically).

If any result but 'Driver or passenger hit' is rolled twice, take the next highest result.

5.5 MECHANISED WALKERS

Since the advent of the Herbert S. Johnson Mechanical Strider in the USA in 1881, the range of both civilian and military variants has multiplied rapidly.

Most factories, mines, docks and construction sites now have these as they exponentially increase a man's strength and ability to use powered tools – one man in a Mechanised Walker can do the work of six men or two strong horses.

The Great Powers were also not slow to see the applications of an armoured version of this invention. Now they can be seen supporting infantry on a hundred battlefields. It was the Walker assault on the barricades that ended the Second Paris Commune in 1887.

Mechanised Walkers are controlled by a 'Steersman' who rides in front, strapped into the control harness. Their arms and legs are linked to control lines that move the Walker's arms and legs. Their hands operate smaller control levers to change gear and operate tools and weapons.

The whole contraption is powered by a steam dynamo attached to the back.

The military versions can be equipped with such weapons as machine guns, Arc cannons or flamethrowers.

The Johnson Mk VII, the 'Worker's Friend'.

Their armour is generally a simple steel plate welded in front of the Steersman, with a vision slit cut into it.

A Walker can move a the full listed speed in one direction. For each turn of 45° or more they lose 1" of speed. Medium and Heavy Walkers can ignore the effects of Type 1 Difficult Terrain on their movement.

Steam Horses. Developed specifically for the US Cavalry, the Cody Steam Horse is an unusual four-legged Walker (see below). It provides its rider with great speed and endurance and is also more damage-resistant (and less temperamental) than a living horse. However, it provides no additional strength, protection or firepower.

If a Walker takes a successful hit, roll on the following table:

1d10	Effect
1–3	Steersman hit – roll Pluck as normal. If it is a knocked down result then the steersman is stunned and the walker ceases to function until he 'gets up'.
4–5	Steering damaged – cannot turn left (4) or right (5).
6–7	Weapon damaged – the owner picks one weapon, it cannot be used again this game.
8	Armour damaged – reduce to armour rating 7.
9	Immobilised – cannot move but can still use weapons.
10	Destroyed – steersman must make Pluck roll to jump free before it explodes.
If any result but 'Steersman hit' is rolled twice, take the next highest result.	

Type	Description	Speed	Armour	Weapons/Tools		Cost
Johnson Mk VII	Light industrial walker	9"	8	Steam Fist		22
Johnson Mk XII Cherokee	Light military walker	9"	11	Steam Fist & machine gun		45
Withall Mk II	Medium industrial walker, used for more dangerous applications	6"	10	Steam Fist		22
Kaiser Wilhelm	Prussian heavy military walker	6"	15	Steam Fist and one of the following: machine gun flamethrower Arc cannon		82 88 89
Jackal	French light military walker	12"	11	Steam Fist & Congreve Rocket Gun		43
Scout	British light military walker	12"	11	Steam Fist & machine gun		48
Bulldog	British medium military walker	9"	12	Steam Fist & machine gun		52
Cody Steam Horse	Unusual four-legged walker	15"	9	No weapons other than what the rider uses. This is mostly used by the US Cavalry		21

Walkers can be equipped with carbide lamps for use at night for an additional 3 points.
The Steersman must be purchased at additional points cost (see Company lists). He can do nothing else while driving the Walker. If he survives the Walker being disabled or destroyed he can bail out and join the fray on foot.

6.0 TALENTS

Many figures in this amazing period have abilities beyond the reach of ordinary men. The Company lists indicate which Talents are most applicable to which figures.

Example: In Captain Napier's Company, Sgt Borrage and his men can buy the Bayonet Drill and Marksman Talents. Sgt Borrage, being a scarred and grizzled old veteran may also buy the Tough Talent.

The infamous 'Tiger Jack' Moran, researching his seminal work, *Heavy Game of the Western Himalayas* (1881).

Talent	Description	Cost
Antivenom	No poison, regardless of type or source, can affect this figure.	5
Bayonet Drill	An infantryman with a bayonet attached to his rifle can use the 'Rifle & bayonet' line of the Weapons table.	2
Berserker	If a Figure with this Talent suffers a Knocked Down result from either Shooting or Fighting, it is not Knocked Down. Instead, it receives a +1 bonus to its Pluck and Fighting rolls. This effect continues until it suffers a second Knocked Down result (at which point it is actually Knocked Down and the Berserker effect ends), or until it is taken out of the game.	5
Cavalryman	The penalty for Shooting from a moving horse is only -2. The Cavalryman also gains a bonus of +1 to Fighting rolls on any turn in which he moved while mounted.	3
Duellist	Choose either a pistol or a type of sword. The figure gets a +2 bonus to Shooting or Fighting rolls with this weapon when facing a single opponent.	5
Engineer	An Engineer can repair damaged technology in the field. This takes one full turn, at the end of which the Engineer makes a Pluck roll. If he succeeds, the equipment is usable again. This includes such items as Walkers, Arc, Edison and Steam-driven equipment. Also, where the option is given, an Engineer may select any type of grenade or rocket grenade – explosive, gas, or Brick Lane Bottle.	5
Erudite Wit	This figure can use pithy one-liners to enrage, distract or amuse its opponents. Enemies within 12" and line of sight suffer a -1 penalty to their Fighting and Shooting rolls when trying to hit this figure.	5
Fanatic	The figure's faith in his cause means that he can re-roll his first failed Pluck of the game.	5
Fearless	Nothing scares this figure. It ignores the effect of Terrifying enemies.	10
Gunslinger	If the figure has two pistols he can split SV between them and thus between two targets (3.3.6.1).	5
Hunter	With a hunting rifle, the Hunter can pick his target from a group of figures in base-to-base-to-base contact with each other. He does not suffer the usual -4 penalty on the attack roll and if he misses there is no chance of him hitting other members of the group.	5
Immortal	Only applicable in campaign games. If the figure is taken out of the game, its post-game survival check (see 3.5.4) determines whether it is available for the next game (Pluck exceeded) or whether it 'sits out' one game while recovering (Pluck equalled or missed). Unlike others, the figure cannot actually die as a result of the post-game survival check.	10
Impervious	This figure cannot be directly affected by Mystical Powers. It would, for example, ignore the effects of Clouding Men's Minds or Spitfire – but neither could it benefit from such Powers as Dragon Wings or Strengthen. Obviously, a figure with this Talent may not also have Mystical Powers.	5
Inspirational	An Inspirational Leader confers a bonus of +1 to the Pluck rolls of all his followers who are within 12" and line of sight of him. This bonus does not apply to the Leader's own Pluck rolls.	10
Intuitive	A figure with this Talent gains a +3 bonus to its Armour the first time it is shot at during the game.	5
Leadership	This is a bonus to Initiative rolls for the Leader of a Company or his deputy. No more than two figures in a Company can have the Leadership Talent. The maximum Leadership score is +3.	3 points per +1
Marksman	Choose a ranged weapon for this figure. When Shooting with this weapon, it ignores cover penalties.	5
Martial Artist	Can Fight unarmed very effectively (using karate, kung-fu, aikido, jiu-jitsu, savate etc.) – see Weapons table. Also gains a bonus of +1 to Speed (note this can result in a Speed of +3 which is otherwise unachievable).	3
Medic	See 3.5.3.	5
Numb	Whether through drugs or mystical forces this figure is inured to pain. He shrugs off the first hit in an engagement, regardless of the Pluck roll result.	10
Stealthy	When this figure is in terrain that provides cover, any Shooting attack against it suffers an additional penalty of -1.	5
Strongman	This figure may carry and fire a heavy (four-handed) ranged weapon unaided (see 5.2.1).	5
Terrifying	Other figures must make a Pluck roll to assault this figure, or to stand their ground if he moves into contact with them (3.2.5).	10
Tough	This figure adds +1 to all Pluck rolls resulting from Shooting or Fighting hits (but not Pluck rolls made for other reasons).	5
Trick Riding	If this figure is the target of a Shooting or Fighting attack while mounted, it can choose whether the attack is made against the rider or the mount (normally the attacker would choose).	5

7.0 MYSTICAL POWERS

Some figures can become Mystics by purchasing Mystical Powers.

During play the Mystic can choose to use one (but only one) of his Powers in each phase of a turn. Most Powers are fairly short-ranged and of short duration. Although the Mystic can only initiate one Power per phase, he may benefit from more than one Power at a time if a Power initiated in a previous phase is still in effect.

To use a Power, a Mystic must first make a Pluck roll. If he fails he can do nothing else during that Phase.

If he rolls a natural 1, he must make a further Pluck roll – if he fails that he is Knocked Down.

Some Powers, especially those that directly affect enemy figures, allow the affected figures a Pluck roll to resist the Power's effects. This is shown in the 'Pluck Roll?' column in the table below. If the target figure equals or exceeds his Pluck, the Power fails to affect that figure.

Power	Range	Duration	Phase	Effect	Pluck roll?	Cost
Clouding Men's Minds	Self	1 phase	Shooting	No-one can get a clear view of the Mystic to Shoot at him unless they are in base-to-base contact with him.	No	8
Dragon Breath	3" radius	1 phase	Fighting	All enemies within 3" believe that they are on fire. They must make a Pluck Roll – if they fail they are Knocked Down.	Yes	14
Dragon Talons	Self	1 phase	Fighting	The Mystic's fighting attacks count as poisoned (see 5.2.4).	No	5
Dragon Wings	Line of sight	1 phase	Movement	The Mystic can grant the power of flight to one of his followers that she can see, or to himself (Jumping 3.2.7).	No	13
Eye of Odin	12"	Instant	Shooting	The Mystic can Shoot a ranged weapon at an enemy figure, even if it is concealed by cover, limited visibility, or if line of sight is blocked. Cover gives the target figure no protection.	No	9
Feet of Lead	12"	1 phase	Movement	All enemy figures in a 6" radius of the designated target point move as if in Type 3 Difficult Terrain.	Yes	16
Harden	Touch	3 turns	Shooting / Fighting	This adds +1 to the Armour rating of the Mystic or a friend that is in base-to-base contact.	No	8
Levitate	Self	1 phase	Movement	The Mystic can rise up to 12" up a building, tree, cliff etc., in addition to his normal movement.	No	5
Mask of Imhotep	Self	1 phase	Movement / Fighting	All enemies consider the Mystic to be Terrifying (3.2.5).	No*	10
Mesmerism	12"	1 phase	Movement	The target figure moves towards its nearest friend. It will Fight if it makes contact, otherwise it will Shoot at that friend. It can take no other actions this turn.	Yes	14
Spitfire	Line of sight	Instant	Shooting	Counts as a ranged weapon with a weapon bonus of +2.	No	21
Strengthen	Touch	3 turns	Shooting / Fighting	This Power adds +1 to Fighting or Shooting rolls for the Mystic or a friend that is in base-to-base contact.	No	9
The Path of Light	Self	1 phase	Movement	The Mystic creates a clear 6" path through an area of Difficult Terrain directly adjacent to himself. He and/or others can move along the path in single file.	No	7
The Path of Shadows	Self	1 phase	Movement	The Mystic moves 12", unhindered by cover, enemies, or even mountains. He must begin and end this movement in an open space. This Power is used instead of normal movement.	No	9
True Grit	Touch	3 phases	Any	The figure touched gains a Pluck attribute of 2+ for the duration of the power.	No	13
Venom	Touch	1 phase	Fighting	One weapon touched becomes poisoned (5.2.4) during this fighting phase.	No	5
Water Bullets	6" radius	Special	Shooting	The Mystic's followers believe themselves to be invincible. They add +2 to their Pluck rolls until one of them is taken out of the game by a bullet. As soon as this happens, their belief evaporates and they all lose the Pluck bonus.	No	18
Zone of Shadows	6" radius	1 phase	Shooting	Shadows swirl in a 6" radius of the Mystic, granting him and anyone else in the radius cover as if in Type 3 Difficult Terrain.	No	13

* The usual Pluck roll(s) relating to Terrifying figures are still required – but there isn't an extra roll just because a Mystical Power has made the figure Terrifying.

Akhenaton and Professor Abir – not to be underestimated.

COST OF POWERS

The table below is to assist you in designing your own Mystical Powers.

Effect	Cost
Minor Power	5
Major Power[1]	10
No Pluck Roll allowed[2]	3
Range: Self or Touch	0
Range: Up to 6"	2
Range: Up to 12"	4
Range: Over 12"	8
Radius effect: 3"	4
Radius effect: 6"	8
Lasts more than one turn	3

1. Generally a Major power causes or prevents serious damage to one or more figures. Other powers are Minor.
2. The 'No Pluck Roll allowed' cost only applies if the Pluck Roll would save the target from the power.

Abir encourages the reluctant cultists, while Akhenaton leads by example.

8.0 THE COMPANIES

In this game each player commands a Company of fine fellows or dastardly villains.

8.1 THE POINTS SYSTEM

Although many players will be happy just to pit their Companies against each other and allow their tactical acumen and courage to win the day, others do like to have a method to finely balance their forces or create their own bold adventurers.

Figure cost = Pluck cost + FV cost + SV cost + Speed bonus (max +2) + Armour cost + Weapon cost(s) + Talent cost(s) + Mystical Power cost(s).

8.1.1 PLUCK COST

Pluck	2+	3+	4+	5+	6+
Cost	16	9	4	2	1

8.1.2 FV & SV COSTS

FV or SV	+0	+1	+2	+3	+4	+5
Cost	0	1	2	4	9	16

8.1.3 WEAPON COSTS

Weapon costs are provided in section 5.2. In case you decide to introduce new or variant weapons into your games, here is the formula for calculating weapon costs:

Weapon cost = 1 + Bonus cost + Range cost + [Pluck penalty x -1]

Weapon Bonus	+0	+1	+2	+3	+4	+5
Cost	0	1	2	4	9	16

Range	12" or less	More than 12"	24" or more	36" or more	48" or more
Cost	1	2	4	9	16

- If a weapon's attack ignores most types of armour add 3 to the cost.
- If it attacks all figures within a radius, or can attack multiple targets, add 3 to the cost.
- If the weapon can only be fired on alternate turns, subtract 1 from its cost.
- If a weapon is poisoned, add 8 to its cost.

8.1.4 ARMOUR COSTS

Armour costs are provided in section 5.1. In case you decide to introduce new or variant armour into your games, here are the costs for each Armour rating:

Armour	7	8	9	10	11	12	13	14	15	16	17
Cost	0	1	2	4	9	16	25	36	49	64	81

- If a particular armour type provides protection against Arc weapons, calculate its points cost for its 'normal' Armour Rating. To this, add half the points cost for its Arc Armour Rating, rounding down. Hence a

Faraday coat has a cost of 5: [normal Armour Rating of 8 = 1 point] + [(Arc Armour Rating of 11 = 9 points) divided by two, rounding down = 5 points].

8.2 FORMING A COMPANY

There are three steps to creating your own Company.

1. Agree a points limit with your opponents. We suggest about 250 points each for a reasonable force.
2. Choose one of the Companies listed in 8.4.
3. Select one figure to be the Leader, then recruit the rest of the Company from the available troops and equipment.

8.3 THE COMPANY ROSTER

Before a game a player must create a Company Roster. This is a list of the figures to be deployed, their equipment and their individual points costs.

The Company Roster should be made available to any opponent who asks to see it.

8.4 THE COMPANIES

Presented in the following pages are a number of Companies for you to choose from. They represent a wide range of types and nationalities from the Steampunk genre. They cover forces from the proud defenders of the British Empire, their chief rivals in Europe (Germany and France), mysterious forces from Egypt and China, and the rising power of the United States. The Company lists below are written to give the maximum flexibility to the players who may wish to use them.

Each list has a table that describes the figures available, along with their attributes, points cost, available talents and basic equipment. Following the table is a range of optional items that fit the Company's theme. The cost given in the Company table includes the listed basic equipment but none of the additional options listed below it.

In a Company you should have a Leader, possibly a deputy leader, one or two specialists and a handful of troops. Ordinary troops are important as they give you the numbers and the breadth of tactical options you will require to win.

Krieg and Kobalt drive their men forward.

Should you wish to create your own forces, these Companies will stand as good models upon which to base them. The key thing is to decide upon a clear theme for your new Company. This will then act as the arbiter for what you should put into it. In the interests of balance we recommend that no more than one figure in your Company has a Pluck of 2+.

8.4.1 A BRITISH RIFLE COMPANY

'To the legion of the lost ones, to the cohort of the damned,
To my brethren in their sorrow overseas,
Sings a gentleman of England cleanly bred, machinely crammed,
And a trooper of the Empress, if you please.'
    Rudyard Kipling, *Barrack Room Ballads*

The Company described below is used in many of the examples throughout these rules. It is led by a Captain of the British Army. He has gathered together a Company of brave men to assist him in hunting down the enemies of the Empire.

Sgt Borrage wades into yet another skirmish.

Type	Pluck	FV	SV	Speed	Cost	Talents	Basic Equipment
Captain	3+	+4	+4	+1	57*	Leadership +2 (May choose up to 2 Talents at additional cost)	SRC breastplate, pistol, sabre
Sergeant	4+	+3	+3	+0	29	Leadership +1	Brigandine, military rifle, bayonet
Rifleman	5+	+2	+2	+0	20		Brigandine, military rifle, bayonet
Field Surgeon	4+	+0	+2	+0	15*	Medic (May choose 1 Talent at additional cost)	Lined coat, pistol
Sapper	5+	+2	+2	+0	47	Engineer	Brigandine, pistol, Congreve Rocket Gun & 4 rocket grenades (any type)
* Not including the cost of any additional Talents							

OPTIONS
- A Captain may replace his pistol with an Arc pistol (+4 points).
- Sergeants and Riflemen may buy explosive grenades (+6 points per grenade).
- Sergeants and Riflemen may purchase the Marksman Talent (+5 points) and/or the Bayonet Drill Talent (+2 points).
- Sergeants may purchase the Tough Talent (+5 points).
- Any figure may purchase a Breath Preserver (+2 points).
- Two Riflemen may exchange their military rifles and bayonets for a pistol each and a machine gun – one fires while the other loads. This team costs 37 points.

This is the Company Roster for basic British Army Companies. However, the army of the Queen-Empress is incredibly diverse with many renowned, unique and characterful regiments. Below are some specific regiments that could be chosen to add colour to your games. You can mix and match men from different regiments in the same Company.

The listings below are for the other ranks – your Captain remains as listed above.

Troops	Pluck	FV	SV	Speed	Cost	Talents	Basic Equipment
Royal Engineers (Sappers)	5+	+2	+2	+0	16	Engineer	Brigandine, pistol **Options** • May buy a Congreve Rocket Gun (+7 points). • May deploy in Scout (+48 points) or Bulldog (+52 points) walkers. • Two men may operate a flamethrower – one fires while the other pumps (43 points for the team).
Ghurkhas	5+	+2	+2	+0	19	May have the Fearless Talent (+10 points) and/or the Stealthy Talent (+5 points)	Jack, military rifle, kukri
Highlanders	5+	+2	+2	+0	20	May have 'Highland Fury' (+3 points per man) which makes them Terrifying when moving into a Fight, but only if one man has bagpipes instead of a rifle (-4 points).	Brigandine, military rifle, bayonet
Royal Welsh	5+	+2	+2	+0	20	May have +1 to Pluck while Fighting (+2 points)	Brigandine, military rifle, bayonet
Sepoys	6+	+1	+2	+1	18		Jack, military rifle, bayonet
Sikhs	4+	+2	+1	+0	20		Jack, military rifle, bayonet **Options** • NCOs may buy a sword (+4 points)
Guards (Grenadier, Coldstream, Irish, Welsh & Scots) or Royal Marines	4+	+2	+2	+0	22	May use SRC breastplate armour (+14 points).	Brigandine, military rifle, bayonet
Blues & Royals	4+	+2	+2	+0	31	May have Cavalryman Talent (+ 3 points).	Breastplate, carbine, pistol, sabre, horse **Options** • May exchange horse for Scout (+43 points) or Bulldog (+47 points) walkers, but note that Cavalryman Talent does not apply to these.

THE PRINCE OF WALES'S EXTRAORDINARY COMPANY

This Company is a unit, based in Horseguards, which has been formed as a quick reaction force to deal with the more 'unusual' events occurring across the Empire. Its members are drawn from across the British Army's many and diverse regiments. They are well equipped with 'normal' weapons and armour, but tend not to have access to the more exotic recent inventions as these take forever to gain Ordnance Board approval. A very promising young officer, Captain Napier, who will often personally lead Sections of the Company into battle, currently commands the Company.

In the rules, many of the examples are based on the exploits of one of these Sections – Captain Napier, Sergeant Borrage, Private Davies and others will be familiar to anyone who reads the whole rulebook.

The bold Captain's normal outfit is himself (Fearless), Sgt Borrage (Bayonet Drill, Marksman & Tough), eight Riflemen (Bayonet Drill & Marksmen), an old Army Surgeon – Dr Wilson (Medic) – and Sapper Jones (Engineer).

8.4.2 THE EXPLORERS' CLUB

'It is a hard thing when one has shot sixty-five lions or more, as I have in the course of my life, that the sixty-sixth should chew your leg like a quid of tobacco. It breaks the routine of the thing, and putting other considerations aside, I am an orderly man and don't like that. This is by the way.'

H. Rider Haggard, *King Solomon's Mines*

This is a prestigious gentlemen's club on the Mall in London. All the greatest expeditions that the British carry out are planned, financed and equipped from here. The men, and a few women, of the club are some of the most talented and courageous that the Empire has to offer.

Type	Pluck	FV	SV	Speed	Cost	Talents	Basic Equipment
Explorer	2+	+3	+4	+1	63*	Leadership +2, Hunter (May choose 1 Talent at additional cost)	Jack, hunting rifle, pistol, bullwhip
Big Game Hunter	3+	+2	+5	+1	60	Leadership +1, Hunter	Brigandine, hunting rifle, pistol, knife
Scientist	5+	+0	+0	+0	10	Engineer	Pistol
Socialite	5+	+1	+1	+0	10*	(May choose up to 2 Talents at additional cost)	Jack, shotgun
Loyal Manservant	4+	+1	+0	+1	20*	(May choose up to 2 Talents at additional cost)	Jack, military rifle, sword
Native Bearer	6+	+0	+0	+2	9		Spear, shield
Rifleman	5+	+1	+2	+0	16		Brigandine, military rifle
Ape Howdah	6+	+5	+0	+0	30	Terrifying	Naturally tough hide – treat as jack armour

* Not including the cost of any additional Talents

OPTIONS

- Any Rifleman may be a Pathan – they can take the Marksman Talent (+5 points).
- Any Rifleman may exchange his military rifle for a shotgun (-4 points)
- Any Native Bearers may be a Zulu – they can take the Fearless Talent (+5 points).
- An Ape Howdah (see 5.4) may be carried by a Silverback with the Tough talent (+5 points) and may be Fearless (+10 points) if carrying a lady.
- A Scientist may purchase an Arc Generator (+20 points). If he does, Explorers and Big Game Hunters may exchange their hunting rifles for Arc rifles (-7 points).

LORD CURR'S COMPANY

This Company is considered both untrustworthy and far too adventurous by most would-be patrons, which means they do get the pick of the most 'interesting' missions.

Lord Edward Ronan Curr, late a Major of the Queen's Own African Rifles, is a maverick. He lost his commission after successfully putting down a Bantu uprising at the cost of most of his command. Lord Curr usually carries a pistol, bullwhip and either an Arc rifle or a double-barrelled Holland & Holland elephant gun. He is an Explorer with Leadership +2 and the Fearless and Tough Talents.

Lord Curr's Company advances cautiously through the Dragon Lady's Limehouse lair.

Lady Felicity, sometimes known as 'Two-Gun Tess', is Lord Curr's constant companion and almost as much of a maverick as he is. She wears normal-looking clothes with the equivalent of a Magneto-static waistcoat built into her bodice. She carries two expensive Italian custom-made pearl-handled pistols, with which she is an expert shot – particularly when firing one in each hand. She is a Socialite and has the Gunslinger Talent.

Mohan Singh is Lord Curr's loyal Sikh manservant, whose massive frame allows him to comfortably fire a machine gun from the hip. He wears either light protection or no armour. He has the Strongman Talent.

'Mad Mick' McFarlane is a brilliant Scottish Engineer, once described by Brunel as 'seriously deranged, but quite possibly a genius'. As with most of the rest of the Company, he favours light protection and his weapons usually consist of an Arc pistol and a variety of grenades. He is a Scientist and has the Engineer and Fanatic Talents.

The foot soldiers of Lord Curr's Company are usually referred to as 'The Incorrigibles'. They are a mixed band of revolutionaries, ex-soldiers, street toughs and other ne'er-do-wells. They are typically armoured in brigandine and armed with military rifles or shotguns, depending on their backgrounds. They count as Riflemen.

Lord Curr also has African native bearers in his service. Typically equipped with spear and shield, they are loyal and quick but often little use in a fight.

Probably the most unusual member of Lord Curr's Company, though, is his mount – a Giant Ape. No-one (with the possible exception of Lady Felicity) knows how he trained this creature to lope along on all fours while carrying him in a howdah on its back. Surprisingly, it has proved utterly loyal – it is also very dangerous in close combat and terrifies his opponents.

Lord Curr and Count Friedrich von Ströheim are old enemies, having crossed swords in Afghanistan, German South-West Africa, Istanbul and New York City.

Type	Pluck	FV	SV	Speed	Cost	Talents	Basic Equipment
Lord Curr	2+	+3	+3	+1	66	Leadership +2, Fearless, Hunter, Tough	Jack, Arc rifle, pistol, bullwhip
Mad Mick McFarlane	5+	+0	+2	+0	40	Engineer, Fanatic	Jack, Arc pistol, grenades x3 (any type)
Lady Felicity	5+	+0	+4	+0	24	Gunslinger	2 pistols, Magneto-static waistcoat (in bodice)
Mohan Singh	4+	+3	+2	+1	36	Strongman	Jack, machine gun, sword
Incorrigible	5+	+1	+2	+0	16		Brigandine, military rifle

OPTIONS
- Any Incorrigible may exchange his military rifle for a shotgun (-4 points)
- Lord Curr may exchange his Arc rifle for a hunting rifle (+7 points)

8.4.3 SCOTLAND YARD

'In another life, Mr Holmes, you would have made an excellent criminal.'
Inspector Lestrade, Scotland Yard, 1894

The most famous police force in the world is London's Metropolitan Police based out of Scotland Yard. In these troubled times, their 'Special Branch' has a number of Companies deployed around the capital to investigate and foil dastardly foreign plots against the city, Parliament and Her Majesty.

Scotland Yard's finest, ably assisted by the Consulting Detective and his colleague, the Good Doctor.

Occasionally they will enlist the aid of a world-famous consulting detective and his able companion, the good doctor.

Type	Pluck	FV	SV	Speed	Cost	Talents	Basic Equipment
Chief Inspector	3+	+2	+3	+0	31*	Leadership +2 (May choose 1 Talent at additional cost)	Brigandine, pistol
Sergeant	4+	+2	+2	+0	18*	Leadership +1 (May choose 1 Talent at additional cost)	Lined coat, pistol, English All-Electric Truncheon
Constable	5+	+1	+1	+0	11		Lined coat, pistol, English All-Electric Truncheon
The Consulting Detective	2+	+3	+2	+1	43*	Erudite Wit, Leadership +2 (May choose up to 3 Talents at additional cost)	Lined coat, pistol
The Good Doctor	3+	+2	+3	+0	27*	Medic, Leadership +1 (May choose up to 2 Talents at additional cost)	Lined coat, pistol
* Not including the cost of any additional Talents							

OPTIONS

- Any Constable may be Special Branch and swap his pistol for a carbine (+2 points).
- Any policeman may use a Steam Carriage (+10 points).
- The Consulting Detective and the Good Doctor may purchase Faraday coats (+5 points) or Vulcan coats (+2 points).
- The Consulting Detective and the Good Doctor may use a Steam Hansom (+12 points).
- Any policeman may buy a Vulcan coat (+2 points). They consider it to be the best protection against Brick Lane Bottle Grenades.
- Any figure may buy a Bicycle (+3 points).

8.4.4 THE SOCIETY OF THULE

'Anyone who has ever looked into the glazed eyes of a soldier dying on the battlefield will think hard before starting a war.'

Otto von Bismarck

This ancient and secretive order of the Holy Roman Empire was founded by Frederick Barbarossa in 1185. For centuries it has used its money and influence to support any who wish to reform the German nation.

Recently it has begun to take a more direct hand under its latest Grand Master, Count Friedrich von Ströheim. The Count has combined an obsession with the occult and Prussian military efficiency to provide strange and amazing weaponry for his followers.

When he takes to the field himself, the Count wears elaborate Prussian military uniform including the classic spiked 'pickelhaube' helmet and (of course) a monocle. The Count lost his left arm in Istanbul when it was shot off by Lord Curr's elephant gun; the missing limb has now been replaced by a remarkable electro-mechanical prosthesis. By way of armour, von Ströheim relies on a Magneto-static waistcoat. His preferred weapons are a classic military sabre and the ultra-modern Mauser machine pistol.

The Society of Thule, on the hunt for rare artefacts in Egypt.

The Count's personal artificer is Dr Kobalt, the twisted genius behind the Tod-truppen. He is short, balding and wears wire-rimmed glasses. Lightly armoured in a long, lined leather coat, Kobalt is nevertheless dangerous to face in battle. He carries both an Arc pistol and an Arc generator. In addition to providing constant power for his sidearm, this generator supplies the energy to keep the Tod-truppen animated – so he is usually surrounded by them.

Feldwebel Krieg is the Count's bodyguard. He has no sense of humour or imagination and is completely loyal, both to the Society and to its Grand Master. In battle he wears brigandine armour and his weapon of choice is a devastating flamethrower.

The Society's foot soldiers start out as elite Prussian infantry (Jägers) wearing lined coats and armed with military rifles and bayonets. If they are lucky, that's how they finish a battle too. However, if they fall in action…

The Tod-truppen are basically zombies. The Society's Jägers go into battle psychically preconditioned and fitted with electro-chemical devices called Revivifiers that re-animate them pretty much immediately after they are taken out. Provided, as noted above, that they are within the field of an Arc generator. In this animated condition they lose their human memories and skills but, in typical zombie fashion, are very difficult to stop with conventional weapons. A side effect of the reanimation process is that the Tod-truppen decay much more rapidly than normal corpses, hence their grotesque appearance. This also means that they are rarely good for more than one battle.

Living Jägers can also be Luft-truppen. These soldiers are suspended by harnesses from something that looks like a small barrage balloon but which they can steer (to a limited extent) across the battlefield. This gives them the advantages of height – a clear view of the battlefield, no issues of difficult terrain, no fear of landmines – but also makes them something of an easy target. Lord Curr's Company refer to them as 'krieg-pigeons'…

The final element in the Society's armoury is less easy to make fun of. It is the Kaiser Wilhelm Heavy Walker. This massive war machine has near-impenetrable armour, attacks with a steam-powered fist and is fitted with either a machine gun, a flamethrower or an Arc cannon depending on the model. The only good news is that these machines are inordinately expensive and even the Society is rarely able to field more than one at a time.

Type	Pluck	FV	SV	Speed	Cost	Talents	Basic Equipment
Thule Kapitan	3+	+3	+2	+0	53	Leadership +2, Fanatic	SRC breastplate, Arc pistol, sabre
Thule Feldwebel	4+	+2	+1	+0	30	Leadership +1, Fanatic, Bayonet Drill	Lined coat, military rifle, bayonet
Von Ströheim	2+	+3	+2	+0	79	Leadership +2, Fearless	Magneto-static waistcoat, Mauser machine pistol (carbine), All-Electric Limb Prosthesis, Arc generator, sabre
Feldwebel Krieg	4+	+2	+2	+0	34	Tough, Strongman	Brigandine, fighting knife, flamethrower
Dr Kobalt	5+	+0	+0	+1	39	Leadership +1, Engineer	Lined coat, Arc pistol, Arc generator
Jäger	5+	+2	+2	+0	26	Bayonet Drill	Lined coat, military rifle, bayonet, Revivifier
Tod-truppen*	3+	+3	+0	+0	n/a	Numb, Terrifying, Antivenom	Lined coat, hands are equivalent to clubs

* A Society of Thule company does not start a game with Tod-truppen. Instead, all its Jägers have Revivifiers. If a Jäger is taken out of the game and is within the area of effect of an Arc generator, he rises as a Tod-truppen at the start of the next turn. Tod-truppen immediately collapse if they are not in the area of effect of an Arc generator, but rise again if one is in range at the start of the next turn. Tod-truppen that are taken out of the game by Fighting or Shooting, however, cannot rise again. They have little intelligence – they discard their weapons and fight with their hands, which are similar to clubs in effectiveness – and cannot run, but they will move and attack in accordance with the orders of any (living!) member of the Society in line of sight. If there is no-one to control them, they will move to attack the nearest enemy – provided this doesn't take them outside the field of an Arc generator. If there is no controller and no reachable enemy, they will fall back and defend the nearest Arc generator.

OPTIONS

- Any Jäger may deploy as Luft-truppen with a Luft-harness (+10 points).
- A single Jäger may discard his military rifle and bayonet and deploy in a Kaiser Wilhelm Heavy Walker. This costs 96/102/103 points depending on what armament is taken for the walker (see 5.5)
- Two Jägers may exchange their military rifles and bayonets for a pistol each and a machine gun – one fires while the other loads. This team costs 49 points.
- Two Jägers may exchange their military rifles and bayonets for a pistol each and a flamethrower – one fires while the other pumps. This team costs 45 points.
- Feldwebels and Jägers may buy the Marksman Talent (+5 points).
- Any Jäger may take explosive grenades (+6 points per grenade).
- Any figure may have a Breath Preserver (+2 points).

8.4.5 THE BLACK DRAGON TONG

'When it is obvious that the goals cannot be reached, don't adjust the goals, adjust the action steps.'
Confucius

The Black Dragon Tong is a secret arm of the Chinese Boxer movement. Its members dwell amongst the Chinese communities in the great cities of the West, using the opium trade and various other rackets to fund their nefarious activities. They are hell-bent on bringing terror to the heart of the governments of the West by targeting senior officials, government ministers and even monarchs and presidents.

In London they are led by the mysterious 'Dragon Lady', who is said to breathe poison and have a fresh Englishman's heart for breakfast every day. Few, even among the Tong membership, can describe her appearance accurately or consistently – there are even rumours that she can change form. The most common description is of a statuesque woman of indeterminate age, dressed in long, flowing, decorated oriental robes and fighting with a deadly combination of unarmed combat skills and Mystical Powers. Her favoured Powers are Dragon Breath, Dragon Talons, Dragon Wings and Water Bullets.

The Dragon Lady's senior lieutenant is Master Wu-jen. He, and a few more junior lieutenants, act as the interface between the Lady and the rest of the tong. Wu-jen is an expert warrior, both unarmed and with his favourite sword. He fights unarmoured but, like the other lieutenants, has the advantage of a few Mystical Powers granted to him by the Lady.

The Dragon Lady, Mistress of the Black Dragon Tong, and her devoted bodyguards.

The Tong can field three types of 'soldier', all driven to some extent by opium addiction. Of these, the toughest is the Dragon Warrior. These heavily tattooed martial artists fight unarmoured, wielding their two-handed swords and halberds with fanatical fervour.

The Tong members are also fanatical, but not as well trained as the Dragon Warriors. They tend to be lightly armoured and fight with pistols and knives or choppers.

The third type of soldier is the Boxer – perhaps best characterised as 'rabble'. They have little in the way of fighting skills, no armour and only archaic muskets and hand-to-hand weapons. There is, however, an awful lot of them and, if inspired by the Dragon Lady's powers, they can fight fanatically to the death.

The most fearsome fighter available to the Dragon Lady is, however, not human – it's a Yeti. These are very rare beasts and she is unlikely to be able to field more than one in any given fight. A Yeti is very tough in close combat and is driven mad with rage when injured – making it even more dangerous to the opposition.

Type	Pluck	FV	SV	Speed	Cost	Talents	Basic Equipment
The Dragon Lady	2+	+3	+0	+2	62	Leadership +2, Martial Artist, 30 points of Mystical Powers	Lined coat
Master Wu-jen	3+	+4	+0	+2	55	Leadership +1, Fanatic, Martial Artist, 20 points of Mystical Powers	Sword
Tong Lieutenant	4+	+2	+2	+0	23	Leadership +1, Fanatic	Lined coat, pistol, fighting knife
Dragon Warrior	4+	+3	+0	+2	24	Fanatic, Martial Artist	Two-handed sword
Tong Member	5+	+1	+1	+0	16	Fanatic	Lined coat, pistol, fighting knife
Boxer	6+	+0	+0	+2	12		Muzzle-loading rifle, club or fighting knife
Yeti	3+	+5	+0	+0	45	Terrifying, Berserker	Thick fur (equivalent to brigandine), talons (equivalent to fighting knife)

OPTIONS

- Any Tong Member or Boxer may have fireworks for use as explosive grenades (+6 points per grenade).
- Dragon Warriors and Tong Members may have a Dragon Tattoo (+10 points) that makes them Fearless.
- A Tong Lieutenant may exchange his pistol for a shotgun (+2 points) or his fighting knife for a sword (+1 point), but not both.

8.4.6 THE SERVANTS OF RA

'My name is Akhenaton, king of kings: Look on my works, ye Mighty, and despair!'

Shelley, paraphrased by Akhenaton

Dedicated to the restoration of the glory of Egypt under the Pharaohs, the Servants of Ra have reincarnated the spirit of the young pharaoh Akhenaton into a willing subject. Unfortunately for them, Akhenaton has his own agenda which (surprise) involves world domination. First, however, he must collect together a number of items of the sacred Regalia of Ra that have been plundered by western antiquarians and are now on display in major museums and private collections. With each successful recovery he becomes more powerful.

Akhenaton dresses in a combination of ancient Egyptian and modern European styles. He wears no physical armour but is well protected by the Regalia of Ra he has recovered so far, his Talents and his Mystical Powers. His only physical weapon is the Khopesh of Osiris, which is part of the Regalia and is itself imbued with Mystical Powers.

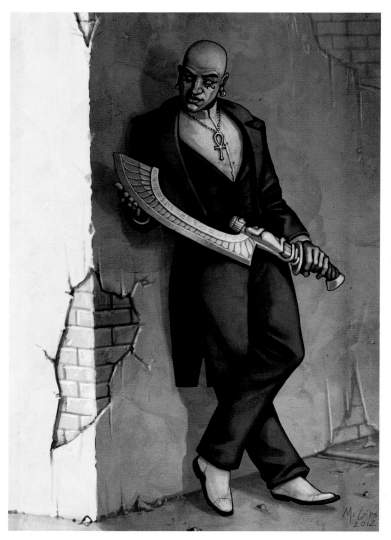

Akhenaton, reincarnated pharaoh.

Supporting Akhenaton is Professor Abdul Abulbul Abir, a fanatical Turkish Egyptologist. He is High Priest of Akhenaton's cult and is responsible for his reincarnation. Professor Abir wears a lined coat and carries no weapons – like his Pharaoh, he relies mainly on Mystical Powers in battle.

The Professor's beautiful daughter Sairah is just as fanatical. She also has a particular hatred of westerners – her mother died in a skirmish with the Légion Étrangère. Sairah is the leader of the cult's drug-addled Syrian Hashashins. She fights unarmoured and lightly dressed, relying on a combination of speed, agility, Mystical Powers and a poisoned fighting knife. Other Hashashins (who can be male or female) have very similar fighting styles but few of them have Mystical Powers.

The young Pharaoh can also call upon the service of his elite Nubian Guard, though they are currently few in number. Their Captain, Ambullah, is a hugely muscled man who wears Breastplate armour and prefers to fight with a two-handed khopesh, though he also carries a Winchester carbine looted after a skirmish with an American Company. Other Nubians tend to use brigandine armour, one-handed swords and shotguns.

The cult of Akhenaton has many followers, but most of them are worth more as worshippers than as fighters. If they do get involved in combat, it is with a motley collection of clubs, knives and pistols.

If Akhenaton is really pushed, the Professor can raise a small number of mummified priests to defend his God-Pharaoh. Like the Prussian Tod-truppen, the Mummies are very hard to put down in a fight. Unlike the Tod-truppen, however, the Mummies fight with intelligence and have Mystical Powers.

Akhenaton and Abir raid an ancient tomb and enslave its occupant.

Type	Pluck	FV	SV	Speed	Cost	Talents	Basic Equipment
Akhenaton	2+	+4	+0	+0	106	Leadership +2, Terrifying, Erudite Wit, 30 points of Mystical Powers	Khopesh of Osiris, Immortal Oil of Horus
Professor Abir	3+	+0	+0	+0	38	Leadership +1, Fanatic, 20 points of Mystical Powers	Lined coat
Ambullah, Nubian Captain	3+	+5	+2	+1	56	Leadership +1, Tough	Breastplate, two-handed sword, carbine
Nubian Guard	4+	+2	+2	+1	25	Tough	Brigandine, sword, shotgun
Sairah	3+	+3	+1	+2	50	Stealthy, Fanatic, 10 points of Mystical Powers	Fighting knife (poisoned), throwing knives
Hashashin	3+	+2	+0	+1	25	Stealthy	Fighting knife (poisoned)
Mummified Priest	3+	+3	+0	+0	46	Terrifying, Numb, 10 points of Mystical Powers	Ancient wrappings (lined coat equivalent), hands are equivalent to clubs
Cultist	6+	+0	+0	+0	3		Club

OPTIONS

- Any Cultist may replace their club with a pistol (+1 point)
- Any Cultist may take a khopesh (sword) (+4 points).
- Any figure with a Leadership bonus may be mounted on a horse (+11 points).

THE REGALIA OF RA

These are the six items that make up the Regalia of Ra. While Akhenaton has only two of these in his possession, the rest make great objectives for a mission or campaign and so are included here.

Regalia	Description	Cost
Khopesh of Osiris	This counts as a sword with a bonus of +2 and a Pluck penalty of -2 as it tries to sever the victim's connection to his immortal soul	5
Immortal Oil of Horus	This sanctified oil is rubbed into Akhenaton's skin before a battle and gives him Armour 13	25
Ramses' Lion Bow	This counts as a hunting rifle in all respects and also grants the user the Marksman Talent	21
Crown of Upper Egypt	This grants the Mesmerism Mystical Power to the wearer, with the extra ability of making two enemies fight one another	25
Crown of Lower Egypt	This is an ancient Electrostatic Burst Generator	15
Amulet of Isis	Applies a Pluck penalty of -2 to anyone attempting to resist a Mystical Power used by the wearer	15

One of the infamous Dooleys.

8.4.7 THE WILD WEST SHOW

'Keep your hands off your guns or there will be more dead men here than this town can afford to bury!'
Wild Bill Hickok

A part of Wild Bill Hickok's famous show regularly tours Europe and the Middle East. Its popularity and renown make it a perfect cover for an American Secret Service Company.

The principal members of this Company are the Dooleys – an extended family of former outlaws who are now trying to earn pardons through their work for the Secret Service. They are expert riders and trick-shooters that know how to provide flamboyant entertainment as well as how to fight for real. Unfortunately, they also like to play with dynamite. This Company is equipped with top-of-the-range American steam-horses.

They are young, rash and enthusiastic, yet remarkably successful. If you need a band of men who can guide a galloping steam horse through busy traffic, firing two pistols at once and whistling Dixie all the while, these are your boys.

They are occasionally supported by a few US Cavalrymen dressed as outlaws.

Type	Pluck	FV	SV	Speed	Cost	Talents	Basic Equipment
Bill Dooley	2+	+3	+4	+1	71	Leadership +2, Gunslinger, Duellist	Lined coat, two pistols, fighting knife, steam horse
Ben Dooley	3+	+4	+3	+1	66	Leadership +1, Gunslinger	Lined coat, two pistols, fighting knife, steam horse
Sioux Ironjaw	4+	+3	+2	+1	41	Trick Rider, Tough	Spear, carbine, horse
Outlaw	5+	+1	+2	+0	39		Lined coat, pistol, military rifle, steam horse
Old Jeremiah, the Mountain Man	3+	+1	+5	+0	55	Hunter, Tough	Hunting rifle, fighting knife
US Cavalryman	4+	+2	+2	+1	27	Cavalryman	Lined coat, carbine, sabre, horse

OPTIONS

- The Dooleys or any Outlaw may take dynamite sticks (treat as explosive grenades)(+6 points per grenade).
- One of the Dooleys may replace his lined coat with a Patent Kelly Suit (+48 points).
- Old Jeremiah may take a Monocular Targeting Array (+7 points).

8.4.8 THE LÉGION ÉTRANGÈRE – 4ÈME BATTALION, LES ZOUAVES DE KREISS

'Nous sommes des dégourdis,
Nous sommes des lascars,
Des types pas ordinaires.
Nous avons souvent notre cafard,
Nous sommes des Légionnaires.'
    Le Boudin, the Légion march

The French Republic has chosen to focus its covert struggles with the other Great Powers through the famous Foreign Legion. As a result, the Legionnaires receive the most modern kit the Republic can provide – and get sent on the most dangerous missions.

The 4ème Battalion 'the Zouaves' has a particular reputation in this field. It is commanded by Col Kreiss and supported by Professor Moebius, a scientist who (assisted by his half-African daughter Amelie) has blended European science and African lore to produce serums that temporarily boost the Legionnaires' fighting abilities.

A Legionnaire is scared of very little and has an improved Pluck attribute compared to most soldiers.

Type	Pluck	FV	SV	Speed	Cost	Talents	Basic Equipment
Col Kreiss	3+	+4	+4	+1	60	Leadership +2, Inspirational	Breastplate, pistol, sword
Sgt Major Baptiste	3+	+2	+3	+0	44	Leadership +2, Tough	Lined coat, military rifle, bayonet
Captain	3+	+3	+2	+1	30	Leadership +2	Lined coat, pistol, sword
Sergeant	3+	+2	+3	+0	31	Leadership +1	Lined coat, military rifle, bayonet
Legionnaire	4+	+2	+2	+1	22		Lined coat, military rifle, bayonet
Professor Moebius	5+	+0	+0	+0	27	Medic	Serums*
Amelie	5+	+0	+0	+0	21	Mesmerism, Medic	Winning Smile?
Bedouin Tribesman	5+	+1	+2	+2	25	Cavalryman	Military rifle, sword

* Prof. Moebius' serums give the men the abilities of various animals:
• The courage of the Lion (+2 to Pluck rolls)
• The speed of the Cheetah (+3" move)
• The eyes of an Eagle (+1 to Shooting rolls)
• The claws of the Bear (+1 to Fighting rolls)
He can give one serum per phase to a figure with which he is in base-to-base contact at the beginning of the Movement Phase. The effects of the serum last until the end of the game. Once a figure has taken one serum it cannot take another during the same game.

OPTIONS

- A Captain may replace his pistol with an Arc pistol (+4 points).
- Captains and Sergeants may buy the Tough Talent (+5 points).
- Sergeants and Legionnaires may purchase the Marksman Talent (+5 points) and/or the Bayonet Drill Talent (+2 points).
- Sergeants and Legionnaires may take explosive grenades (+6 points per grenade).
- Any figure may have a Breath Preserver (+2 points).
- Two Legionnaires may exchange their military rifles and bayonets for a pistol each and either a machine gun or an Arc cannon – one fires while the other loads. This team costs 41 (machine gun) or 38 (Arc cannon) points.
- A single Legionnaire in the Company may replace his military rifle and bayonet with a pistol and the Medic Talent (-4 points).
- Any Legionnaire may become a Zouave and be equipped with a Vertical Spring Translocator (+8 points).
- Any Legionnaire may discard his military rifle and bayonet and deploy in a Jackal Walker (see 5.5) (+31 points).
- Any Bedouin Tribesman may be equipped with a horse (+11 points).

8.4.9 THE BRICK LANE COMMUNE

'This is the final struggle
Let us group together, and tomorrow
The International
Will be the human race.'
The song of the Internationale

For the poor, the late Victorian period was a time of virtual slavery in the 'dark satanic mills' or the Workhouse. It was a short step for a man to take to become a member of one of the many revolutionary and republican movements of the day.

In London the centre of much of this burning resentment is Brick Lane in the East End. Exiled Russian and German intellectuals give these desperate men a cause to fight for – class war! Like their comrades in the Paris Commune, most Incendiaries are women. Anarchists are more often men, but also include a fair number of women, boys and girls. Though poorly armed and ill equipped, the Brick Lane Anarchists make up for it in numbers and hatred.

Type	Pluck	FV	SV	Speed	Cost	Talents	Basic Equipment
Working Class Hero	3+	+2	+1	+2	40	Fearless, Leadership +2	Lined coat, military rifle
Political Commissar	2+	+1	+1	+1	41	Leadership +1, Fanatic, Revolutionary Rhetoric*	Lined coat, pistol
Anarchist	4+	+1	+0	+1	8		Club
Incendiary	4+	+0	+1	+1	24		Brick Lane Bottle Grenade x3

* Unique Talent: Revolutionary Rhetoric (10 points; included in Political Commissar cost)
If any of the opposing companies has a member of the Nobility or a Military Officer in their number the Brick Lane Anarchists and Working Class Hero get +1 bonus to their Fighting and Shooting rolls when targeting that hated symbol of the Bourgeoisie.

OPTIONS

- Anarchists and Incendiaries may buy the Fanatic talent (+5 points each).
- Any Anarchist may replace his club with a fighting knife (+1 point) or a shotgun (+3 points).
- Any figure may buy a Bicycle (+3 points).
- A single Anarchist may discard his club and deploy in a Withall Mk II Industrial Walker (see 5.5) (+20 points).

8.4.10 THE US MARINE CORPS

'From the Halls of Montezuma, to the shores of Tripoli;
We fight our country's battles, in the air, on land, and sea;
First to fight for right and freedom, and to keep our honor clean:
We are proud to claim the title, of United States Marine.'
   The Hymn of the United States Marine Corps

The toughest troops the President of the United States has to offer. They are often used in foreign missions where reliability (not something for which the Dooleys are renowned) is necessary.

Type	Pluck	FV	SV	Speed	Cost	Talents	Basic Equipment
Captain	3+	+4	+4	+1	43	Leadership +2	Brigandine, pistol, sabre
Gunnery Sergeant	4+	+3	+3	+0	29	Leadership +1	Brigandine, military rifle, bayonet
Marine	5+	+2	+2	+0	20		Brigandine, military rifle, bayonet
Navy Corpsman	5+	+0	+1	+1	13	Medic	Jack, pistol
Navajo Scout	5+	+1	+2	+2	36	Hunter, Stealthy	Hunting rifle, fighting knife

OPTIONS

- A Captain may replace his pistol with an Arc pistol (+4 points).
- Any Captain, Gunnery Sergeant, or Marine may be equipped with a Rocket Pack (+5 points).
- Captains and Gunnery Sergeants may buy the Tough Talent (+5 points).
- Gunnery Sergeants and Marines may purchase the Marksman Talent (+5 points) and/or the Bayonet Drill Talent (+2 points).
- Any Marine may discard his military rifle and bayonet and deploy in a Johnson Mk XII Cherokee Walker (see 5.5) (+33 points).
- A single Marine may replace his military rifle and bayonet with a pistol and a Congreve Rocket Gun (-2 points). Rocket grenades (explosive) must be purchased separately (+7 points per grenade).
- Any Marine may have explosive grenades (+6 points per grenade), and may also carry ammunition (explosive) for the Congreve Rocket Gun (+7 points per grenade).
- Any figure may have a Breath Preserver (+2 points).
- One figure may carry an Edison Beam Translator (+25 points).

9.0 SCENARIOS

Although you could just play head-to-head across some terrain, carrying on until only one Company has any figures left in the game, it is often more pleasing to have an agreed scenario to play with specified terrain, objectives and/or victory conditions.

This adds a whole new set of tactical considerations and leads to a much more satisfying evening's entertainment. Below are some examples of what you could include in your games.

9.1 STANDARD SCENARIOS
9.1.1 OBJECTIVES

Pieces of new technology, a secret formula, invasion plans, code books, gold and diamonds etc. These must be collected by the Companies and taken off the table at their entry point. A single figure cannot carry more than one objective.

SET-UP 1

1. Set up the terrain as described in section 4.1.6.
2. Place three counters along the centre line of the table. No objective should be within 9" of another.
3. Deploy as normal.

SET-UP 2

1. Set up the terrain as described in section 4.1.6.
2. Place six counters within 12" of the centre point of the table. No objective should be within 4" of another.
3. Three of the counters are dummies (mark the underside with a 'D').
4. Deploy as normal.

VICTORY

- 2 Victory Points (VPs) per enemy figure taken out of the game.
- 5 VPs per enemy Leader taken out of the game.
- 20 VPs per objective recovered and safely removed from the table.

9.1.2 BRING HIM BACK ALIVE

A VIP is lost in no man's land and must be rescued or captured and returned to the Company's entry point.

SET-UP

1. Set up the terrain as described in section 4.1.6.
2. Place the VIP in the centre of the table.
3. Deploy as normal.

Kreiss finally has Akhenaton right where he wants him.

VICTORY

- 2 VPs per enemy figure taken out of the game.
- 5 VPs per enemy Leader taken out of the game.
- 20 VPs if the VIP is recovered and safely removed from the table.
- 10 VPs if the VIP is taken out of the game while in enemy hands.

9.1.3 LAST MAN STANDING

A real grudge has been building between the Companies, and now is the time to finish it.

SET-UP

1. Set up the terrain as described in section 4.1.6.
2. Deploy as normal.

VICTORY

- When all enemy figures are taken out of the game.

A Dragon Warrior, one of the Black Dragon Tong's elite fighters.

9.1.4 BREAKTHROUGH

One Company must get at least one man from one table edge to the other, and the other Company must stop them.

SET-UP

1. Set up the terrain as described in section 4.1.6.
2. The defending Company deploys first, up to 12" into the table from their starting edge.
3. The breakthrough Company deploys as normal.

VICTORY

- 2 VPs per enemy figure taken out of the game.
- 5 VPs per enemy Leader taken out of the game.
- 20 VPs for the defending Company if no enemy slip through.
- 5 VPs per figure the breakthrough Company manages to get off the opposite table edge.

9.1.5 MARKED FOR DEATH

Each Company has been hired to kill the Leader of the other side.

SET-UP

1. Set up the terrain as described in section 4.1.6.
2. Deploy as normal.

VICTORY
- The game ends at the end of the turn in which a Leader is taken out of the game. Note that this could result in a draw if all Leaders die in the same turn.

9.1.6 FORT NIL POINT
A vital building or position must be held until reinforcements arrive. One Company defends, the other(s) attack.

SET-UP
1. Set up the terrain as described in section 4.1.6, except that there must be a building or ruin in the table's centre.
2. The defending Company must set up in the building in the centre of the table.
3. The attacking Company deploys as normal.
4. The game lasts for 12 turns, at which point overwhelming reinforcements arrive for whichever Company is in control of the central building.

VICTORY
- 2 VPs per enemy figure taken out of the game.
- 5 VPs per enemy Leader taken out of the game.
- 20 VPs for the Company in control of the central building at the end of turn 12.

9.1.7 DEATH AT YOUR HEELS
Soon this area will be devastated by a rolling artillery barrage or a natural disaster such as lava flows or rising floodwater. The only hope is to get to a Steam Launch waiting at the riverbank. The Launch only has room for one Company.

Outnumbered, the Society of Thule occupies a defensive position in a ruined church.

SET-UP

1. Set up the terrain as described in section 4.1.6, except that one table edge is the river bank.
2. The Steam Launch is at the centre of the river edge.
3. The Companies deploy along the opposite edge to the river at least 6" apart.
4. From the second turn onwards the area of devastation rolls forwards from the deployment edge by 1d10-2". This happens at the end of the Movement Phase and any figure caught by it is out of the game.

VICTORY

- 2 VPs per enemy figure taken out of the game.
- 5 VPs per enemy Leader taken out of the game.
- 5 VPs for each figure saved by getting on the Steam Launch.

9.1.8 KING OF THE HILL

A vital building or position must be taken and held against all comers.

SET-UP

1. Set up the terrain as described in section 4.1.6, except that there must be a building or ruin in the table's centre.
2. Deploy as normal.
3. The game lasts for 12 turns, at which point overwhelming reinforcements arrive for whichever Company is in control of the central building.

VICTORY

- 2 VPs per enemy figure taken out of the game.
- 5 VPs per enemy Leader taken out of the game.
- 20 VPs for the Company in control of the central building at the end of turn 12.

9.1.9 CATCH THE PIGEON

A courier pigeon is sitting in the centre of the table. It is carrying a vital message. Each turn it will move 1d10-2" in a random direction. Companies can capture it by moving into contact with it, or by shooting it and then moving up to it. If it moves off the table both Companies lose.

SET-UP

1. Set up the terrain as described in section 4.1.6.
2. Deploy as normal.

Type	Pluck	FV	SV	Speed	Talents	Basic Equipment
Pigeon	6+	n/a	n/a	+3		Small and nimble! (Armour 10)

VICTORY

- 2 VPs per enemy figure taken out of the game.
- 5 VPs per enemy Leader taken out of the game.
- 20 VPs for the Company that captures the pigeon and returns to its deployment point with it.

9.1.10 BAD JACK

A mutated laboratory experiment has escaped and is stalking the table killing anyone it comes across. The Companies must hunt it down.

SET-UP

1. Set up the terrain as described in section 4.1.6, except that there must be a building or ruin in the table's centre.
2. Deploy as normal.

Type	Pluck	FV	SV	Speed	Talents	Basic Equipment
Bad Jack	2+	+4	n/a	+2	Berserker, Fearless, Terrifying, Tough	Thick hide (Armour 10)

VICTORY

- 2 VPs per enemy figure taken out of the game.
- 5 VPs per enemy Leader taken out of the game.
- 20 VPs for killing Bad Jack.

9.2 SCENARIO COMPLICATIONS

Adding one of these can turn a scenario upside down. Obviously some complications will not apply to certain landscapes. For example an Earthquake will not affect anyone on a Dirigible.

Agree with your fellow players if you want to add a complication and then either choose one or determine which one randomly.

9.2.1 ACHTUNG MINEN!

It turns out that the battlefield has been mined by unknown saboteurs. Each turn any figure moves, it may activate a mine. Roll 1d10 at the end point of its move – on a 1 it has stepped on a mine. It must make a Pluck roll with the usual results of being Knocked Down or taken out of the game. Mechanised Walkers are immune to mines, as are Luft-truppen.

Startled civilians flee from a sudden Prussian raid.

9.2.2 PEA SOUP

A dense fog has descended over the battlefield. At the beginning of each turn, roll 2d10. The sum of the two dice scores is the visibility distance in inches for the rest of the turn. You may not fire at any figure beyond that distance. If you roll a double 1 or a double 10 the fog lifts.

9.2.3 COLLATERAL DAMAGE

There are lots of civilians on the battlefield. Every time you miss, roll the attack again and on a modified score of 10 or more you have injured or killed a civilian. If you kill more than a dozen civilians, you have lost the game, regardless of any VPs acquired, as your patrons will no longer reward you.

9.2.4 TWILIGHT

The light is fading fast. At the beginning of the game you can see 24". At the beginning of each turn, that distance decreases by 1". You may not fire at any figure beyond that distance unless they are standing within a lit area (e.g. illuminated by a streetlamp, carbide lamp or storm lantern).

9.2.5 THE AUTHORITIES

By the end of turn 6, the noise of the battle has attracted unwanted attention from the local Authorities. A Chief Inspector, a Sergeant and six Constables from Scotland Yard (or the local equivalent) will arrive in the centre of a random table edge equipped as shown in 8.3.6. they will move towards the closest figure and begin making arrests.

If there are multiple figures, they will break up into two sections – one led by the Chief Inspector and the other by the Sergeant. They will continue until the game ends or they are all taken out of the game.

The Chief Inspector will have the Fearless Talent and the Sergeant the Tough Talent.

Any figure that they take down will be considered to be unconscious, not dead, and handcuffed to the terrain.

9.2.6 QUAKE

An earthquake has begun. Every turn, at the beginning of the movement phase roll 1d10 – on a 1 or 2 a tremor occurs. Anyone still in a man-made structure such as a building or ruins takes a hit at the end of the movement phase and must roll Pluck to survive. If they get a Knocked Down result, they are trapped in the building and cannot move but can still Shoot and be shot at.

9.2.7 THE CLOAK OF NIGHT

Many subversive activities are best carried out at night. This changes the battlefield considerably. Unless you have a source of light, or your target is illuminated, your line of sight is restricted to just 1". At the beginning of the game, agree with your fellow players all the sources of light on the battlefield. These could be street lamps, lamps over doorways, the light coming from windows, burning braziers by the watchman's hut etc.

Figures using Rocket Packs, Vertical Spring Translocators and the like always count as landing in Difficult Terrain unless they land in an illuminated area or have light sources of their own.

10.0 LANDSCAPES

The world is incredibly diverse and offers a wide range of landscapes across which your Companies can do battle. Each landscape has a number of unique features that give various advantages and disadvantages to the competing Companies. The following are some examples of what you could choose to create.

Combining a Landscape, a Scenario (9.0) and perhaps one or more Scenario Complications (9.2) gives you nearly a thousand different games to play. This also gives you a huge range of game types to use together to form narrative campaigns if you wish.

Akhenaton's reach stretches even to the cow towns of the American West.

10.1 CITY STREETS BY DAY

The modern Victorian city had broad avenues and narrow side streets overshadowed by buildings up to six stories in height. It was a busy place often choked with horse drawn and steam driven traffic, bicycles, hawkers, religious and political pamphleteers, beggars, pickpocketing gangs etc.

Benefits: Daylight

Hazards: Collateral damage rule applies (9.2.3). May quickly attract the attention of the Authorities (9.2.5). In London, Aberdeen or New York you could add Pea Soup fog (9.2.2) to the mix.

Suggested Terrain: Buildings set out along roads, possibly civilian vehicles that move along preset paths (4.1.5 Dangerous Terrain).

10.2 CITY STREETS BY NIGHT

At night the streets take on a very different character. Out come the prostitutes and their patrons. The theatres and the opera are open, so we have the well-heeled mixing with the scum of humanity. Civilians are more likely to be armed.

Benefits: Line of sight and ranges are reduced favouring short-ranged weapons.

Hazards: Poorly lit. Only the main streets will have a good number of lamp posts. In other areas, you may have to rely on the lights by pub doorways or outside better appointed residences giving you pools of light. In London in particular you could add Pea Soup fog (9.2.2) to the mix.

Suggested Terrain: Buildings set out along roads, a few civilian vehicles.

10.3 COURTYARDS AND ALLEYWAYS

Crowded, dimly lit and where bad things often happen. No respectable citizen would wander here from the main streets unless they had business to conduct. Remember to think in three dimensions as there may be exterior stairs, windows, loading doors with pulley hoists up the side of the buildings.

Benefits: Plenty of cover.

Hazards: Limited entry points, restricted space to manoeuvre, limited cover. A bit of a slaughterhouse.

Suggested Terrain: Narrow roads surrounded by buildings, connecting small open spaces.

10.4 THE DOCKS

The heart of the great Victorian city was often its docks. This is where commerce, both legal and less so, was done. There will be warehouses, goods being offloaded, cranes, ships and slipways.

Benefits: Plenty of cover from warehouses, stacks of goods being offloaded, cranes, ships, slips and wagons (both horse and steam).

Hazards: Collateral damage rule applies (9.2.3). May quickly attract the attention of the Authorities (9.2.5). Lots of moving goods vehicles (4.1.5).

Suggested Terrain: The river or seafront down one table edge and then fill the rest of the board with buildings, vehicles, people, goods etc. Docks tend to be less organised than streets so you can be more random in the placement of features.

10.5 THE CITY PARK

A relatively new introduction to many cities of the time. They were often busier than they are now and had more open spaces. People of all classes liked to promenade along the paths, meet friends for lunch and so on. Parks often had exhibitions, fairs or circuses in them.

Benefits: Clear lines of sight.

Hazards: The Collateral damage rule may apply (9.2.3). May quickly attract the attention of the Authorities (9.2.5).

Suggested Terrain: Clumps of trees, small buildings such as cafes. workmen's huts, glasshouses.

10.6 OVER THE ROOFTOPS

A dangerous landscape, popular in films. A variety of roof types from steeply pitched to flat may be used.

Lord Curr's Company head down to the docks in pursuit of their foes.

Benefits: No civilians or Police.

Hazards: Think of the word 'plummet'. Anyone Knocked Down has a chance of sliding off and thence to their doom. Give a figure that is Knocked Down just one chance to recover. After that they are out of the game.

Suggested Terrain: Buildings with a variety of pitched and flat roofs at differing levels. There will be solid brick chimney stacks on every building. Between the buildings will be gaps of various widths. Allow figures to leap a gap that is half their movement rate as long as the rest of that movement is the run up before the jump.

10.7 THE FACTORY

No Victorian city would be complete without factories large and small, full of rows of heavy machinery

Benefits: Plenty of cover.

Hazards: Possibly hazardous machines and combustible materials. Half of all terrain must be Dangerous (4.1.5). The Collateral damage rule may apply (9.2.3).

Suggested Terrain: A series of large chambers with lots of machines, stacks of goods, carts, pillars, stairwells etc.

10.8 A NIGHT AT THE THEATRE

A meet goes wrong and suddenly a crowded theatre becomes a slaughterhouse full of screaming patrons and gunfire. Or a rendezvous in the deserted building turns ugly with double crossers ambushing the Company from the balconies and boxes.

Benefits: Good sight lines across the theatre.

Hazards: The Collateral damage rule may apply (9.2.3). May quickly attract the attention of the Authorities (9.2.5).

Suggested Terrain: An open space surrounded by a stage and balconies.

10.9 THE GREAT MUSEUM

This was the age when the imperial nations plundered the cultural wealth of poorer and savage nations to display to an admiring public. It is a classic place to have objectives (9.1.1).

Benefits: Plenty of cover.

Hazards: May quickly attract the attention of the Authorities (9.2.5).

Suggested Terrain: A series of large chambers with lots of display cabinets and exhibits.

10.10 THE OLD CEMETERY

London, Rome, Vienna and Paris have large, densely 'populated' public cemeteries, full of graves, crypts and mausoleums.

Benefits: Plenty of solid stone cover.

Hazards: During the day, or if there is an interment taking place the Collateral damage rule may apply (9.2.3). There is also the chance of meeting less savoury visitors such as body-snatchers and the like. Very poor lighting at night.

Suggested Terrain: Rows of headstones, crypts, mausoleums, small copses of trees and dense undergrowth, divided by narrow paths.

10.11 THE CATHEDRAL

An oasis of calm in a troubled city, the Cathedral draws the faithful to it. The Cathedral is also often used as neutral ground for meets between conspirators and other parties.

Benefits: Plenty of good cover.

Hazards: During the day, the Collateral damage rule may apply (9.2.3).

Suggested Terrain: Pews, altars, crypts, confessionals, columns etc.

10.12 THE SHUNTING YARD

In the centre of every great city is a shunting yard where the Railway Companies move and load goods, and tend to engines, wagons and carriages.

Benefits: Reasonable cover, which might unfortunately move about. Few civilians, especially at night.

Hazards: Dangerous Terrain (4.1.5) such as tank engines shunting rolling stock about.

Suggested Terrain: As above, plus water towers, coal heaps, signal boxes, engine sheds etc.

10.13 THE PATHAN VILLAGE

Beyond the Khyber Pass are some of the most inhospitable territories on earth, where the British and Russian Empires play 'The Great Game' at the gateway to India.

Benefits: None to speak of.

Hazards: Heavily armed natives, dust, heat, flies and an untimely death all await the unwary.

Suggested Terrain: Mud-brick compounds, wells, dry ditches.

10.14 THE STEAMER

The trade of empires and nations travels the globe in the holds of these rugged craft.

Benefits: The enemy has nowhere to escape, but then again, neither do you.

French sniper, pride of the Republic!

Hazards: Going overboard is probably fatal. Throwing grenades about near the hull could doom you all.

Suggested Terrain: Open decks, gantries, cranes, open holds, the bridge, mast etc.

10.15 THE ORIENT EXPRESS

A truly classic cinematic battleground where warring Companies could create absolute carnage. Do not forget running along the roof.

Benefits: Excellent service, great accommodation.

Hazards: Restricted space to manoeuvre. Falling out or off can be fatal. On the roof there are low bridges and other hazards to consider. The Collateral damage rule will apply (9.2.3).

Suggested Terrain: Pretty obvious.

10.16 THE HINDENBURG

The pride of the Prussian civilian dirigible fleet and the most advanced airship in the world.

Benefits: None. This is a very bad place to fight.

Hazards: Restricted space to manoeuvre. Dangerous Terrain (4.1.5) in the form of huge, inflammable Hydrogen gas bags. Long, long drops.

Suggested Terrain: The passenger decks resemble those upon the Orient Express. Then there are the service ways between the gas bags.

11.0 THE CAMPAIGN

An Adventuring Company's work is never done, and it's rare that an operation doesn't lead into another thrilling mission. This simple system allows players to link scenarios together into an ongoing campaign for their Companies. As with all elements of the game, the Golden Rules apply.

A campaign is a linked series of encounters based upon a story. These allow a group of players to find more meaning in their exploits than they would in single games.

Lord Curr and 'Mad Mick' prepare for battle.

The story should go through three main phases:
- The opening encounters
- The middle game
- The Finale

In the opening encounters the players should compete for clues, and learn the capabilities of the enemies that they are facing. By the time they get to the middle game the Companies should have advanced and become leaner and meaner, and greater prizes for success should be offered. In the middle game there should be plenty of one-on-one games across a variety of landscapes as the Companies progress towards the Finale. This should be an all-out game involving every Company, possibly played across an entire afternoon and on a large table.

11.1 RANDOM MISSIONS

As part of the above you could randomly generate scenarios and the landscapes over which they are fought. Rolling on these sample tables will give you a good start for an urban-focused campaign but you can create your own Scenario and Landscapes tables to suit the type of campaign you wish to play and your available terrain:

d10	Scenario
1	Objective (9.1.1)
2	Bring him back alive (9.1.2)
3	Last man standing (9.1.3)
4	Breakthrough (9.1.4)
5	Marked for death (9.1.5)
6	For Nil Point (9.1.6)
7	Death at your heels (9.1.7)
8	King of the Hill (9.1.8)
9	Catch the Pigeon (9.1.9)
10	Bad Jack (9.1.10)

d10	Metropolitan Landscapes
1	City Streets (10.1/10.2)
2	Courtyards & Alleyways (10.3)
3	The Docks (10.4)
4	The City Park (10.5)
5	Over the Rooftops (10.6)
6	The Factory (10.7)
7	The Great Museum (10.9)
8	The Old Cemetery (10.10)
9	The Cathedral (10.11)
10	The Shunting Yard (10.12)

Prussian Tod-truppen, serving in death.

11.2 SURVIVAL

It is a sad fact of life for the Adventuring Companies that some don't make it home. Use the Post-game Survival Test (3.5.4) to see if figures taken out during a scenario manage to recover. Of course, figures that were taken out during a scenario may, depending on how the game went, have been taken prisoner by the enemy and their rescue could form a later scenario in the campaign.

11.3 THE SPOILS OF WAR

Over time, characters can acquire new skills and abilities, or may invest in new equipment. Any VPs awarded during a scenario may, between games, be spent on advancing and developing the Adventuring Company that earned them.

Quite simply, each VP earned provides 1 point that may be spent on equipment from the Armoury (5.0), Talents (6.0) and Mystical Powers (7.0), or improving characters' attributes (8.1).

Only equipment options available to a figure (see the Company lists – 8.4) may be purchased. For example, a British Army Sergeant may buy an explosive grenade – he may not, however, purchase a Kaiser Wilhelm heavy walker.

Talents and Mystical Powers work a little differently. Figures may choose any Talent, provided they can afford it, though it is recommended that a character-appropriate reason be given – for example, the scars received by Sgt Borrage in his recent encounter with the Black Dragon Tong have left him with a Terrifying visage. Only figures with existing Mystical Powers (or with the option to take them) may purchase further powers.

Attributes may be increased by paying the points costs listed in 8.1. For example, it costs 16 points for a character with Pluck 3+ to improve to Pluck 2+, and a figure with FV +3 can improve to +4 for 9 points. Note that all costs must be paid to advance more than one level – to improve from Pluck 4+ to Pluck 2+ costs 25 points (9+16), not just 16 points. Players may also spend VPs to buy new figures for their companies. Such figures must, of course, be drawn from the original Company lists.

The Légion clashes with the Society of Thule.

IN HER MAJESTY'S NAME – REFERENCE SHEET

TURN SEQUENCE

1. INITIATIVE

Roll 1d10 and add Leadership. Re-roll ties.

2. MOVEMENT

Figures in Heavy Armour lose their Speed bonus (if any).
Figures in Medium or Heavy Armour cannot Run
Any figure already engaged in a Fight cannot move other than to Disengage (3.2.4).
A figure may be moved in any direction.
Its movement may be slowed by the terrain (4.1).

Type	Base Speed	Difficult Terrain?
Ape Howdah	9"	No effect on Movement
Bicycle	9"	No
Edison Beam Translator	n/a	No
Horse	12"	Yes
Luft Harness	4"	Ignores
Rocket Cycle	18"	No
Rocket Pack	12"	Ignores
Shanks' Pony (foot)	6" + Speed	Yes
Steam Carriage	9"	No
Steam Hansom	12"	No
Ornithopter	9"	Ignores
Electro-trike	12"	No
Vertical Spring		
Translocator	12"	Ignores

Type	Speed	Armour
Johnson Mk VII	9"	8
Johnson Mk XII Cherokee	9"	11
Withall Mk II	6"	10
Kaiser Wilhelm	6"	15
Jackal	12"	11
Scout	12"	11
Bulldog	9"	12
Cody Steam Horse	15"	9

3. SHOOTING

Roll 1d10 + SV + Weapon + other modifiers.

Common Shooting Modifiers	Modifier
Shooting at a target that moved 3"+ this turn	-2
Shooting at a target that has Run this turn	-3
Shooting if you have moved in same turn	-4
Shooting at a target that is in a Fight	-4
Volley fire: each additional shooter adds	+1
Target is in Difficult Terrain (Type 1/2/3)	-1/-2/-3

4. FIGHTING

Roll 1d10 + SV + Weapon + other modifiers.

Common Fighting Modifiers	Modifier
If you outnumber an opponent	+1
Mobbing: each additional fighter adds	+1

PLUCK ROLLS

Each time a figure is hit make a Pluck roll immediately. This roll may be modified if attacker's weapon has a Pluck Penalty.
If the result is greater than Pluck, figure is OK.
If the result is equal to Pluck, figure is Knocked Down.
If the result is less than Pluck, figure is out of the game.
A natural, i.e. unmodified, roll of 1 is always a failure, a natural roll of 10 is always a success.

Fighting Weapons	FV Bonus	Pluck Modifier
Axe	+1	-1
Axe (large)	+2	-2
Bullwhip	+0	-1
Club	+1	+0
English All-Electric Truncheon	+1	-1
Improvised weapon (small)	+0	+1
Improvised weapon (large)	+0	+0
Knife	+1	+0
Knife (combat or fighting)	+1	-1
Military rifle & bayonet *	+3	-1
Nightstick	+2	+0
Quarterstaff	+3	+0
Rapier	+1	-1
Sabre/Sword	+2	-1
Spear	+2	-1
Steam fist / claw	+4	-3
Sword (large) or Halberd	+3	-2
Unarmed (basic)	+0	+1
Unarmed (Martial Artist)	+1	+0
* requires Bayonet Drill Talent		

Armour	Weight	Rating	vs Arc weapons
Breastplate, SRC	Medium	12	
Breastplate, steel	Medium	11	
Brigandine	Light	9	
Chain shirt, steel	Light	10	
Faraday coat	Light	8	11
Faraday shield	-	+1	+3/+6
Jack / Lined Coat	Light	8	
Magneto-static projection barrier	-	10	
Magneto-static umbrella	-	+2	
Magneto-static waistcoat	Light	9	
None, just clothing	Light	7	
Patent Kelly Suit	Heavy	15	
Plate armour	Heavy	13	
Shield	-	+1	
Vulcan coat	Light	8	

Shooting Weapons	SV Bonus	Pluck Modifier	Range
Arc cannon	+1	-3	24"
Arc pistol	+1	-1	6"
Arc rifle	+1	-2	18"
Blunderbuss	+3	-2	6"
Bow	+2	+0	12"
Carbine	+2	+0	18"
Congreve Rocket Gun	+3	-1	18"
Crossbow	+2	-1	18"
Flamethrower	+2	-1	9"
Grenade (Brick Lane Bottle)	+0	-1	3+SV"
Grenade (explosive)	+0	-1	3+SV"
Grenade (gas)	+0	-1	3+SV"
Hunting rifle	+4	-2	36"
Improvised thrown weapon	+0	+1	3"
Machine gun	+5	-2	30"
Military rifle	+3	-1	24"
Muzzle-loading rifle	+3	-1	18"
Pistol	+1	+0	9"
Shotgun	+2	+0/-1	12"
Shotgun, short	+2	+0/-1	9"
Thrown axe	+1	-1	6"
Thrown knife	+1	+0	6"
Thrown spear	+2	-1	9"